How to Pass the ARE © Michael Riscica 2015

Version 1.0

All rights reserved.

For information about obtaining permission to reprint or repost material from *How to Pass The ARE* or YoungArchitect.com, send your request by email to mikeriscica@gmail.com

Dedication

This book is dedicated to everyone who has graduated from architecture school and has the dream of becoming a Licensed Architect.

Table of Contents

Dedication 1
Thank You 4
Introduction 5
Single User Download 8

Part 1 - Introduction
    Creating Your Own Magic Bullet 10
    What This Book Is and Isn't 13
    How to Use This Book 14
    Resources 15

Part 2 - The Basics
    What Is the ARE 17
    Getting to This Point The ARE Requirements 22
    Confidentiality of the Exam 24
    The ARE 5.0 Transition 26

Part 3 - The Mental - Should I Take the Exam—or Not?
    The ARE vs. Graduate School 30
    Ten Good Reasons Not to Get Your Architecture License 32
    Ten Good Reasons to Get Your Architecture License 38
    Visualize the Possibilities 40

Part 3 - The Mental - Mentally Preparing for the Exam
    The Mental Shift 44
    Commit to Showing Up 46
    Be Prepared to Sacrifice 48
    Seek Others Out 50
    Understand How You Learn 58
    Focus on Yourself ... Not Others 54

Part 4 - The Studying
    The Momentum Concept 56
    Creating Good Energy 62
    Choosing a Testing Order 65
    Creating a Study Schedule 69
    Finding a Study Space 77

Study Materials 80
Practice Exams 87
Flashcards 91
Beating the Vignettes 94
Hacking the MC Questions 103

Part 5 - Taking The Test
Test Day Tips 109
Reading ARE Test Scores 113
Failing the Exam 117

Part 6 - Arriving
Now That You're Finished 125

Thank You

I am deeply grateful for the following people, without their help this book and YoungArchitect.com would not have been possible:

Molly Riscica, Robert J. Riscica, Bob Potter, Tom Johnson, Matthew White, Charles Van Winckle, Lukas and Nicole Argyros, Jamie O'Brien, Edythe and Buddy Kane, Lisa Buffington, Jamie Teasdale, Nick Loper and every person from the SHNIC, Alex Barker, Jeanne Grabowski, The YoYoYogi Community, BNI Portland, The City of Portland, Merryman Barnes Architects, Ryan Hansanuwat, Jared Smith, David Doucette, Jeff Echols, Mark R. LePage, Lora Teagarden, Meghana Joshi, Sean Sheffler, NCARB, AIA, AIAS, Fancy Hands and most importantly everyone who has read and supported YoungArchitect.com

I love you guys.

Introduction

Congratulations!

You're obviously considering taking the Architecture Registration Exam (ARE), or you're in the middle of it.

The fact that you have arrived at this point is no small accomplishment. I think just being eligible to take this test is something worth being proud of. You have clearly been working at your career for many years.

I am honored to help you get a better understanding of what it means to complete the ARE.

It was really important to me personally that I became a Licensed Architect so I could move on with my career and my life. I'll assume you are as serious as I was when I began the process many years ago.

Why I wrote this book

When I took the exam, there was very little information available that wasn't a Ballast or Kaplan text book. I really struggled to figure out how to get past these seven exams. No one was really talking about how to take and study for the ARE.

The ARE Forum was around when I tested, which has since been removed from the Internet. On the Forum, it was really easy to have a dozen people point out what you did wrong on your vignette, but no one was really talking about the exam or what worked for them.

Actually, I take that back. These conversations were happening, but since the conversation on the Forum moves so fast, the threads that were helpful were often impossible to find.

The National Council of Architectural Registration Boards (NCARB) wasn't much help either. Sure, NCARB has made significant improvements to helping candidates study in the past few years. But when I was testing, they provided very little insight and spoke of the exam like it was no big deal, and everyone should be passing it in 6 months to a year. Which certainly wasn"t my story.

I wanted to write a blog

Toward the end of the exams, the light at the end of the tunnel was getting brighter and brighter. I decided that after it was all over, I wanted to start learning about the Internet and blogging.

I like to write, and many years ago, I wrote two blogs about bicycling across the United States. Those blogs were a huge success. However, being in architecture school, dealing with the recession, and taking the ARE prevented me from doing much writing, blogging, and playing on the Internet.

After I completed my exams, I immediately transitioned from studying into blogging at **YoungArchitect.com**. The site went live in January 2014. After I wrote a few blog posts about the ARE, I got an enormous response. Tons of ARE candidates emailed me, thanking me for sharing a few tips and tricks I had figured out when I took the exams.

I started out only wanting to write a few blog posts about the ARE, but each time I did, my readers kept asking for more.

So I gave it to them and just kept going with it. I reviewed the study guides, breaking down how I thought about the exam and sharing all my failures (which ultimately led me to completion). I just went on and on and on about the ARE.

The Blog vs. This Book

After a lot of writing about the ARE, one of my mentors said to me:

> "You should take all this ARE content and format it into a book to sell."

Immediately, I didn't like the idea because I was essentially giving it away for free on my Web site. Why would anyone buy a book? However, his logic was:

> "Sure, this content is free on your site, but by creating a cohesive book, you're removing a lot of the work from the reader—having to go and read 30 different blog posts instead of making it into one convenient product."

This made sense to me. When I took the exam, time was my most valuable resource.

So that's what this book is. Sure, some of the content and ideas are available for free on **YoungArchitect.com/ARE**.

However, most of it it isn't. I wrote a significant amount of content that **isn't on the blog** just for the book. Even the content that came from the blog has all been edited, revised, moved around, and polished for the purposes of this book.

There is also a significant amount of content on the blog that isn't in the book. Some information is better kept on the blog than in this book, such as ARE 4.0-specific information, which will become outdated in a few years when the test transitions to ARE 5.0.

This is a book about studying, not technical content. At the time of writing this book, the details of the ARE transition have not been announced. My goal was to write a book that would still be very relevant after the ARE 5.0 transition. I lived through the transition from ARE 3.1 to ARE 4.0. I know that studying for ARE 5.0 will be very much the same as studying for ARE 4.0.

I truly thank you for making the purchase of this book. Arriving at being a Licensed Architect was incredibly important to me, and I assume it is for you as well. I hope to provide you some value and prevent you from the goose chase that I went on.

You have already started winning if you are reading this!

Michael Riscica, AIA

All content in this book is copyrighted and protected under the US Copyright Act of 1976 and all other applicable international, federal, state and local laws and all rights are reserved.

Much of the content in this book is based on the personal experience of the author. Although the author has made every effort to confirm the accuracy of all content, what is considered accurate today might not be accurate tomorrow. Accordingly, the author assumes no responsibility if your experience differs from his.

Any trademarks, product names, or other relevant features are assumed to be the property of their respective owners.

© 2015 Michael Riscica. All rights reserved

Part 1
Introduction

Creating Your Own "Magic Bullet"

Everyone always wants the magic bullet, the cliff notes, the "four-hour work week," or the easy way to get ahead by doing the least amount of work for the greatest return.

Unfortunately, there is no magic bullet with the ARE. For me, it was approximately 1,000 hours of studying and working toward this goal.

However, as I took the exams from 2009 to 2013, I watched many, many people come and go, but I saw very few people actually finish. Almost all of those people who didn't complete the process were much smarter and more talented (and in a few cases, even better looking) architects than me.

So why did I complete the process, and so many didn't?

After writing this book and a ton of blogposts and talking to a million people about the ARE, I truly think the essence of passing the ARE boils down to mastery of four concepts. I struggled with all of these concepts at one time or another throughout the process. After I got a handle on them, I started to succeed with the ARE.

The four concepts are:

1. **Maintaining consistency**
2. **Dealing with setbacks**
3. **Learning how you learn**
4. **Learning how to study**

Let me explain.

Maintaining consistency means showing up over and over and over again—day after day, year after year after year. Taking the ARE requires a huge time commitment. Some people pass it faster than others. But I'm a slow reader, and it took me awhile to understand many of the concepts well enough that I could take a test about them. Eighty percent of the battle is the ability to say, "I would love to hang out this weekend, but I need to study." Not many people can do that.

I think maintaining consistency is the most important concept. Most people who want to be Licensed Architects but aren't are not willing to show up and put in the work.

Dealing with setbacks means coming back after you've studied your butt off and failed the test anyway. I know many people who took one exam, didn't study hard enough, failed, and never returned. Even I failed the structures exam, got really upset, and wasted two years crying about it.

It means coming back after a life-changing event happens in the middle of the ARE process, like a job loss, a death in your family, or having a kid. These types of things are inevitable. Something like this will happen during any multi-year goal that any of us embark on.

I believe that the only way to truly "fail" the ARE is to not return after you receive a "Not Passing" grade, or after some other life event gets in your way. True failure is not becoming an architect because something external became an obstacle on your path, after you already invested many years of your life into it.

Learning how you learn means paying attention to the act of studying. There are a million books to read, tons of advice to take, and many things to look at. But at the end of the day, all that really matters is what works to help you pass the test—and not everything will work.

In this book, I talk a lot about how me, myself, and I studied for the ARE. I do this because I wish someone shared with me what they did and how they used their time while they were preparing for and taking the exams. I also hope that hearing about my experience gives you insight into a different way of doing things.

Learning how to study means using your time and resources wisely while figuring out how to be a good test taker. After spending a lot of time with the ARE, I realized that college hadn't really taught me how to study for this type of test. Yes, I learned all of the fundamentals necessary to become an architectural intern, but I hadn't learned how to pass tests at the level of the ARE.

Studying for the exams gave me the real world architect education that I needed. It forced me to learn all the boring topics that I didn't learn in school. Sure, the content isn't easy reading. It's really boring at first, but once I got past resisting it and started sipping the Kool-Aid, I started enjoying the material.

The four concepts of **maintaining consistency, dealing with setbacks, learning how you learn, and learning how to study** make up your "magic bullet" to pass the ARE.

I believe that **anyone** can pass this test if they master these four concepts. I'll say that again: I think anyone can pass this test. It doesn't matter how good of a designer you are, what happened in architecture school, BARCH, MARCH, 4-year, 5-year, no architecture degree, CADD expert, very experienced, minimally experienced—**anyone** can pass this test with the right mindset. It's not rocket science; it"s just a lot of damn work.

In the following chapters, I come back to all of these concepts, and several others, in a wide variety of ways. But in my personal opinion, understanding these four concepts is fundamental to passing the Architect Registration Exam.

What This Book Is—and Isn't

What This Book Is

This book includes:

- Study techniques.

- A very big overview of what the exam is to someone who is unfamiliar with the process.

- Sharing some of the mindsets I adopted to help me think about the exam in a more constructive way.

- Identifying very common pitfalls encountered by ARE candidates who never complete the process.

- A collection of tips, tricks, and hacks that I used to help me finish the ARE. I've provide a framework of what worked for me, so you could use that as a starting point to customize your own personal approach to the exams. This will help provide a better understanding of what the exams are, aside from what NCARB tells you.

What This Book Isn't

This book is not:

- A technical book. There are already thousands of technical books that do a much better job of teaching the technical information than I ever could. This book will not teach you how to design a handicap ramp.

- A promise to help you pass the exams in some arbitrary amount of time. Everyone is on a different journey. It took some people two weeks to study for an exam, while I spent much more time.

- A resource to teach you how to do the calculations.

- Technical data to memorize right before an exam.

- A promise to deliver a result that is completely out of my control.

How to Use This Book

This book was written for everyone taking the ARE. More specifically, I wrote this book with the following two people in mind:

1. The ARE candidate who is just beginning the licensing process.
2. The ARE candidate who has struggled and is frustrated with their experience taking the exam.

The chapters and sections in this book are not necessarily intended to be read in order. If you see a chapter or a section that is directly relevant to your current experience with the ARE, feel free to jump ahead or skip around. In other words, I encourage you to read chapters or sections independently of any other material. Read what you think might improve your test-taking or study experience, and save the rest for later.

When I wrote this book I broke it down into five different sections:

- **Basics**
- **Mental**
- **Studying**
- **Taking the Test**
- **Arriving**

The basics section is about the specifics of the ARE, including its history and revisions.

The mental section is about getting your head straight before you start doing any work.

The studying section breaks down all the nuts and bolts of how I studied for the exams.

The test-taking section is about how to get through the actual exam and its aftermath. .

The arriving section is about arriving at the destination of being a Licensed Architect.

Resources

Throughout this book, I mention references on the Internet like study guides, links to specific documents on the NCARB website, and other various topics.

To make it easy for both of us, I built a Web page at:

YoungArchitect.com/AREBook

This Web page provides links to anything I refer to on the Internet. This will save you a lot of time since you won't have to go to a bunch of different place to look things up.

Part 2
The Basics

What Is the ARE?

The Architect Registration Examination (ARE) is developed and maintained by the National Council of Architectural Registration Boards (NCARB). The purpose of the exam is to assess the knowledge, skills, and abilities of ARE candidates. It is accepted by all 50 states in the U.S., as well as 11 provincial and territorial architectural associations for architectural registration in Canada. The ARE is a grueling and challenging exam with an average pass rate of 67 percent on all seven sections.

The exam is broken into seven exams. Many years ago, the entire exam was administered in one day, but today all seven exams take 33.5 hours to complete.

Taking the ARE is a self-guided process. Everyone studies on their own and schedules their own test dates when they feel they are ready to take the exam. Passing all seven exams requires significant preparation, dedication, and a whole lot of discipline.

The History of the ARE

In the early days, the architecture exam was developed and managed by individual state boards. The tests were developed and scored by practicing architects, educators, and specialists in other disciplines. This process lacked uniformity because each state had a different board, which used its own testing guidelines, questions, and standards. From a national standpoint, there was no standard to follow.

NCARB was formed to create more standardization of the ARE and to assist architects practicing architecture in multiple states. A syllabus of written examination subjects, test lengths, and dates of administration were identified. This provided consistency in exam questions and scoring.

Standardized testing became available in the 1950s, and the NCARB converted the ARE syllabus into multiple choice questions. These questions were then made available to all state NCARB boards.

An extensive review of the exam was completed in 1979 and resulted in a general outline of today's ARE. The early ARE consisted of nine divisions taken over a four-day period. The exam was only offered yearly in major U.S. cities. The 1980s brought along new technology that allowed the NCARB to develop a computer-based exam. The last paper test was taken in 1996.

The Seven Exams

The ARE is administered in Prometric testing centers and includes seven different tests. The entire exam includes 555 multiple-choice questions and 11 vignettes. Below, you will find my summary of the subject matter that is included in each exam. I've tried to cover the major subject areas, but I encourage you to do a careful review of NCARB"s ARE Study Guides for a more thorough description. To save you a few clicks, I've included a link to each study guide on my Resources page at **YoungArchitect.com/AREbook**.

Construction Documents and Services (CDS)

The content of the **CDS** multiple choice exam consists of:

- Developing, evaluating, coordinating, organizing, and laying out construction drawings and details, project manuals, and specifications.

- Project delivery methods, Owner-Architect agreements, Owner-Contract agreements, general conditions of the contract, supplementary conditions, business organizations, office organizations, legal issues, and project management.

- Construction administration, construction sequencing, scheduling, evaluating costs, bidding, value engineering, submittals, changes in the work, field administration, progress payments, records management, conflict resolution, and closeout.

- Building Codes, ADA, and health and life safety.

- Content from PPP and SPD will also appear on this exam. I recommend reviewing those chapters or study guides as well.

Programming, Planning and Practice (PPP)

The content of the **PPP** multiple choice exam consists of:

- Urban design, community design, land analysis, transportation influence, climatic influence, social and economic influences.

- Adaptive reuse, space planning and hazardous materials/conditions.

- Historic structures, predesign services, programming, scheduling, legal issues, and project management.

- LEED/Sustainability.

- Building Codes, ADA, and health and life safety.

- Content from CDS and SPD will also appear on this exam. I recommend reviewing those chapters or study guides as well.

Site Planning and Design (SPD)

The content on **SPD** multiple choice exam consists of:

- Site analysis, topography, climate, drainage, utilities, parking, landscaping, property descriptions, adaptive reuse, and material calculations.
- Human comfort, sustainable design, hazardous materials/conditions, psychometrics, lighting/fixtures/furniture/equipment, and air quality.
- Soil, earthwork, shoring and bracing, and site improvements.
- Building codes, ADA, and health and life safety.
- Content from CDS and SPD will also appear on this exam. I recommend reviewing those chapters or study guides as well.

Schematic Design (SD)

This division requires you to complete two very complicated vignettes in building layout and an interior layout with furniture. This section has no multiple choice questions. The total time allotted for this section is six hours.

The first vignette is an interior layout that meets a lengthy list of program, code and ADA requirements. The second vignette is a floor plan of a building that meets many programmatic and code requirements. Some people like to think the SD exam is just one big video game.

Structural Systems (SS)

The content of the **SS** multiple choice consists of:

- Understanding loads, equilibrium, determinate and indeterminate structures, properties of sections, statics, forces, moments, stress, diaphragms, and trusses.
- Basic structural systems, foundations, and soils.
- Structural steel design.
- Structural wood design.
- Structural concrete design.

- Seismic and wind forces.
- Building codes, ADA, and health and life safety.

Building Systems (BS)

The content of **BS** multiple choice consists of:

- HVAC, human comfort, alternative energy sources, energy efficiency, indoor air quality, recycling and reuse, life cycle cost analysis, LEED, and other rating systems.
- Plumbing design, water systems, sanitary drainage and venting, storm drainage, and fire protection.
- Electrical, power supply, lighting, fire alarm systems, moisture protection, building codes, ADA, and health and life safety.
- Content from PPP and SPD will also appear on this exam. I recommend reviewing those chapters or study guides as well.

Building Design and Construction Systems (BDCS)

The content of the **BDCS** multiple choice consists of:

- Soil, earthwork, shoring and bracing, and site improvements.
- Concrete, formwork, vapor barriers, and masonry.
- Steel and metals.
- Wood.
- Structural and rough carpentry, finish carpentry, moisture protection, roofing, flashing, sealants, doors, windows, glazing, and finish materials.
- Elevators, escalators, and ramps.
- Space planning, lighting, sustainability, indoor air quality, hazardous materials/conditions, and building systems.
- Building codes, ADA, and health and life safety.
- Content from SPD and BS will also appear on this exam. I recommend reviewing those chapters or study guides as well.

What Order Do I Take the Exams In?

Many people question which order is best to take the exams. There're a lot of theories out there and a lot of contrasting opinions about ARE testing order. But at the end of the day, it doesn't really matter. Much of the study material in the ARE feeds on itself. I recommend everyone takes the exams in the order that they are most comfortable with. I talk about this in detail in Choosing a Testing Order.

Eligibility

ARE eligibility is managed by the candidate's state or provincial registration board. Most U.S. jurisdictions require that a candidate earn a degree from a professional program accredited by the National Architectural Accrediting Board (B.Arch or M.Arch), as well as meet the experience requirement by completing the Intern Development Program (IDP).

Because each jurisdiction has its own requirements, it is important to review those set forth by your own jurisdiction. A full list of requirements for specific jurisdictions can be found on NCARB's Web site. See the Resources page for a link to that information.

Getting To This Point

If you are reading this book, you have already achieved much success by arriving at this moment in time.

Simply being eligible to sit for the Architecture Registration Exam is a huge accomplishment. For one reason or another, most architecture graduates never actually make it this far in the architectural licensing process. Completing the ARE is just as much work as getting another degree. In some ways, it is much harder, due to the self-guided element of it. I didn't realize this until toward the end of the process.

If you're willing to purchase a book called "How to Pass the Architecture Registration Exam," I am going to make a few assumptions about who you are:

- You are an architecture graduate.
- You have either completed IDP or are working on it right now.
- You are most likely working in an architect's office.

To sit for the ARE, there are two main requirements:

1. **Education**—You must have earned an accredited architecture degree, which takes 5-7 years.
2. **Experience**—You must have at least 5,600 hours of documented on-the-job experience, under the supervision of a Licensed Architect.

This process is lengthy and is no easy feat. However, it is not impossible, and the rewards you can reap by becoming a Licensed Architect are numerous.

The Educational Requirements

For licensure in most states, a candidate must hold a professional degree in architecture from an institution accredited by the National Architectural Accrediting Board (NAAB). There are currently more than 100 architecture schools to choose from.

Right now, there are three different professional architecture degrees available:

- The Bachelor of Architecture (BArch) requires a minimum of 150 credit hours in professional studies and electives.
- The Master of Architecture (MArch) degree requires a minimum of 168 credit hours, 30 of which must be graduate level.
- The Doctor of Architecture (DArch) requires a baccalaureate degree or 120 undergraduate credit hours, in addition to a minimum of 90 graduate credit hours.

The Experience Requirements

The Intern Development Program (IDP) represents a program designed to aid architecture students in learning and developing within the work force. Most states require that a student complete this type of internship before they can become licensed in that state.

The IDP is a thorough and comprehensive program that requires experience in several different settings. Its purpose is to ensure that architecture graduates gain the professional experience, knowledge, and skills needed to practice effectively as independent architects. The intern architect is closely supervised by a Licensed Architect or professional in another discipline.

Interns most commonly work within architecture firms, where they begin to become familiar with the application of their education. They may assist in design projects, prepare documents, research specific building codes, and be involved in many other tasks.

The IDP requires the completion of 3,740 field experience hours within 17 different categories. The experience hours are documented by the intern and then discussed with and signed off by the supervisor. This information is submitted to NCARB on a regular basis.

Confidentiality of the Exam

NCARB doesn't mess around with the security of the Architectural Registration Exam (ARE). Time and time again, as you take the exams, you are constantly reminded from NCARB about the confidentiality of the ARE. Disclosing any information that you see on the exam is strictly prohibited.

The questions on the ARE are designed to test the competency of protecting the health, safety, and welfare of the public. **By disclosing the content of the exam, NCARB views it as you jeopardizing the health, safety, and welfare of the public, as well as the entire reputation of the profession itself.** For many states, the ARE is the very last stop before having an Architect stamp.

The 2009 Cheating Incident

All hell broke loose in 2009. I had just started studying for my first exam. Apparently on The ARE Forum, people were disclosing detailed information that they were seeing on the exam. The ARE Forum is a Web site where ARE candidates would go to chat about studying, help each other with vignettes, or discuss the profession.

NCARB took serious action against eight ARE candidates for violating the confidentiality agreements. They canceled several of their test scores and gave them all 3-4 year suspensions from taking any ARE's.

Enough content on the exams was given away that several sections were unavailable because they needed to be redeveloped. NCARB uses an extremely lengthy process of developing questions for the exam and claims that they lost approximately $1.1 million on administration and legal costs from this incident. To recover, **they passed the costs onto all the ARE candidates by raising each test from $170 to $210.** Due to this incident, the ARE Forum received a lot of bad publicity just because of a couple of bad seeds.

There is nothing wrong with using the forums to study. You just need to be clear about helping vs. cheating. NCARB sees the difference between helping and cheating as follows:

NCARB defines **Helping** as:

1. Sharing what study guides are used
2. Discussing concepts and highlighted information in study materials
3. Reviewing graphic solutions and noting obvious errors
4. Supporting each other and celebrating each other's successes

NCARB defines **Cheating** as:

1. Identifying terms or concepts contained on the exam
2. Sharing answers to questions you had seen on the exam
3. Referring others to "check out" information you saw on the exam
4. Identifying program items from the vignettes
5. Asking others to post information that has been removed from the ARE Forum due to it being illegal

I don't disagree with NCARB's stance on the issue and the rules that they have set in place. Having studied for all seven exams, there is a ton of latitude in discussing the exam without breaking any of the rules. You just have to be careful of what you say and how you say it. NCARB is like the CIA—they're always watching.

The crazy thing is that even after the 2009 incident, I would still sometimes see people posting questionable information on the forums. **Please be careful sharing information on the Internet, in person, or anywhere, especially after you have taken the exam.** If what you need to write or say is questionable, then don't do it.

Let me spell it out for you … Do not take a test and then post what you saw on the exam (how many calculations there were, types of questions, etc.) on the forums. For your own sake, just leave it alone.

The ARE 5.0 Transition

"The only thing that is constant, is change."
– Heraclitus

The Architect Registration Exam is going through a huge change. In 2013, the NCARB Board of Directors approved the development of ARE 5.0, the new and updated version of ARE 4.0. With this new exam, upcoming candidates can expect changes to the structure of the exam, as well as the exam's testing method.

What's changing?

The new version will apply changes that testing candidates should be aware of. One of the primary and most obvious changes is the reduction of divisions. The existing ARE 4.0 consists of seven divisions, including:

- Construction Documents & Services
- Programming, Planning & Practice
- Site Planning & Design
- Building Design & Construction Systems
- Structural Systems
- Building Systems
- Schematic Design

The new ARE 5.0 will consist of six divisions, which will include:

- Practice Management
- Project Management
- Programming & Analysis
- Project Planning & Design
- Project Development & Documentation
- Construction & Evaluation

The method of ARE 5.0 testing is still being determined. The NCARB is investigating new technology that will allow for graphics throughout the exam, new performance-item questions, and other exam improvements. Additionally, the current graphic vignettes will most likely be changed by this new technology. **The exam is not expected to be simpler or more difficult; it will employ different methods of asking questions.**

Why are they doing this to me?

The ARE is continually being evaluated to ensure that the exam remains relevant to current practice. With this evaluation, NCARB considers new testing methods as they become available. Technology has allowed for recent breakthroughs in graphic testing methods. These breakthroughs may be used in ARE 5.0, although nothing has been announced yet.

Improved testing methods will allow for a better determination of a candidate's competency, which is the ultimate goal of the ARE. The ARE is designed to test a candidate's competency to ensure the health, safety, and well-being of the public. NCARB is expecting that better testing technology will evaluate candidates at higher levels of cognition and analytical thinking, similar to the regular practice of architecture.

Additionally, the ARE upgrade was strongly recommended, based on the results of the 2012 NCARB Practice Analysis of Architecture. The new division structure will better align with the more common activities of professional architecture. The new exam version is being developed with the input of architects across the country. All of these varying backgrounds will help ensure that the exam reflects the broad aspects of current practice.

When is this happening?

ARE 5.0 is not expected to launch until 2016. There has been a timeline of events leading up to the rollout of this new version.

NCARB voted in February 2013 to develop ARE 5.0, but the division structure and test specification was not announced until December 2013.

NCARB announced the ARE 5.0 transition plan in May 2014 and intends to release interactive tools to help candidates manage this transition in 2015.

In early 2016, ARE 5.0 study materials will be released, and the launch of ARE 5.0 is expected in late 2016.

On June 30, 2018, ARE 4.0 will be retired. That means the clock has already started for getting in and getting out before ARE 4.0 is retired.

What do I need to do?

Step 1. Chill out! It is too early to really understand the details of how the exam will change.

Step 2. Keep studying.

It is important that you finish the CDS, PPP, and SPD. Focusing study efforts to pass the CDS, PPP, and SPD is the strategy recommended by NCARB for candidates who think they may transition to ARE 5.0. **If you pass these three divisions, you will only need to take two division in ARE 5.0**: Project Planning & Design and Project Development & Documentation. Following this track could lead to the completion of the ARE in five divisions.

Dual delivery of ARE 4.0 and ARE 5.0 will last 18 months. This means that both exams will be offered at the same time. Candidates starting in ARE 4.0 will have 18 months after the launch of ARE 5.0 to finish ARE 4.0 before they are forced to transition to ARE 5.0. Yes, that is a mouthful. Essentially, if you do not complete ARE 4.0 in the 18 months after 5.0 is launched, you will have to complete 5.0. Candidates have the opportunity to test in ARE 5.0 after its launch, if they choose. However, if they transition to 5.0, they must finish in 5.0.

Pay attention to updates put out by NCARB about the launch of ARE 5.0. There will be plenty of information available as the exam is further developed. Don't allow the rollout of ARE 5.0 to intimidate you. Keep studying, and make it a goal to not become a victim of the 5.0 transition.

This book will be updated to reflect the changes in ARE 5.0 that I can address. And, you can always turn to **YoungArchitect.com** for a variety of blog posts about the transition.

Part 3
The Mental

Should I Take the Exam—or Not?

The ARE vs. Graduate School

I graduated with a 5-year B.Arch. After graduation, I moved to the West Coast and got a job with a great firm. Around November, I started to miss architecture school. I tried to keep my mind busy with hobbies like cooking, racing bicycles, and even brewing beer. That worked for a little while, but I really wanted nothing more than to go back to school and continue on with my demented architectural party. Unfortunately, my undergraduate student debt made that virtually impossible.

I was not a happy camper the day I did the math and couldn't get the numbers to work out and allow me to get more education.

Graduate school is very expensive.

Becoming a Licensed Architect is a fraction of the cost of graduate school.

However, you are still signing up for a never-ending commitment to paying NCARB, state boards, continuing education, and AIA fees. All the fees after you are licensed can be a tax deduction, but unfortunately I am not an accountant, only an architect. Here's what it boiled down to for me:

B.Arch + Masters Degree = You're still called an Architectural Intern.
B.Arch + IDP + ARE = Architect

What about teaching?

You need a Master's degree to teach. This frustrated me because I always wanted to go back to architecture school as a professor.

Many universities acknowledge licensure as an appropriate qualification to teach. **Because we do want licensed architects teaching the next generation of architects. Right?!?!**

Changing Direction.

A very pivotal conversation happened for me one day when I was talking to my mentor/old professor/old boss about my petty, post-architecture-school, pre-recession problems. He very honestly said to me:

> **"You don't need any more architectural design education. If you're going to get more education, study something like making money. Why don't you go after getting your Architect License? The license will be significantly more valuable than a Master's degree, and you already have the right degree (B.Arch) to start taking the exams."**

Shortly after this conversation, I got on the path toward becoming a Licensed Architect.

My Logic.

Getting licensed gave me an opportunity to channel my energy and figure out what life was like outside the insulated bubble of academia. More importantly, I think getting licensed really helped me understand and develop a love for the profession.

I write this only to share my experience. I don't think one is better than the other. If I had the opportunity to get more education, I would jump at the chance. But I didn't, so I found something else to do.

I truly believe there is incredible knowledge and information to be gained by completing the licensing process, and I have tremendous respect for everyone that has completed it or is in the process of completing it.

Ten Good Reasons Not to Get Your Architecture License

For me personally, I had to complete the journey of becoming a Licensed Architect no matter what I did. It was hugely important to me to finish what I started. Not having my architecture license was blocking me from advancing my life and career. I needed to close the "becoming an architect"" chapter. **But that's my story. It may not be your story.**

I don't think everyone should become an architect.

In fact, I truly believe that not taking the AREs may be the very best decision for you and your life, depending on who you are. Each of us have had very different lives and upbringings. The decisions I have made with my life, which I knew were right for me, may very well be the worst decisions for you and your life. And vice versa.

Often, we get on this path of going to college and getting a job, and we are led to believe (from NCARB, employers, and society) that getting an architecture license is the next step. I agree with that logic if you actually want it and plan to use it. A message that I think many young architects is missing is that **you don"t NEED to have an architecture license to have a successful career**.

There are some fantastic reasons to not go through the architecture licensing process or to avoid it all costs. Passing my AREs involved many inglorious hours of showing up, sitting in a Starbucks, and reading boring books while all my friends were out partying and having fun.

My intention with this chapter is to achieve one of two things:

    1. Knock you off the fence if you are undecided.

    or

    2. Validate the decisions you have already made, regardless of what they are.

So here are 10 great reasons NOT TO become a Licensed Architect

1. You don't need the closure.

This was my biggest reason for completing the exam. Having that silly piece of paper that said "Licensed Architect" was deeply important to me. I needed to reach that milestone to justify and bring closure to many years of insanity that I put myself through so I could move on with the next chapter of my life.

Getting closure may just not be important to you. **You can still have an extremely successful architecture career without having the architecture license.** You love architecture; you enjoy your work and don't feel the need to prove yourself to you or anyone else. To you, the license is just not important.

Maybe it's important to your company, your boss, or someone else that you get your license. All the work it takes to get that piece of paper isn't about them. It"s really about you.

2. There are other things going on in your life.

Architecture was a lot of fun to study and has brought you a wonderful career. But deep down inside, there are other things that are more important to you than investing massive amounts of time into getting an architecture license. Maybe it's having a child or raising a family, pursuing a hobby, or just going after something else in life.

Don't get me wrong—all of these things are still completely possible. In fact, I have watched many people raise a family at the same time that they became a Licensed Architect, with incredible focus and vigor. **Having the architecture license just may not be that high on your list of life priorities. That's completely ok.**

3. You do not want the responsibility.

When you are an Architect of Record, there is an incredible amount of risk and responsibility involved every time you stamp a drawing. **Meanwhile, changes happen and corners are cut on the jobsite in the name of a contractor's profit.** It's impossible to be on top of everything all the time.

I have recently seen two architects get sued merely because they're the first point of contact and protocol. What they were being sued for was evidently the work of the contractor not following the drawings. Yet the architects still had to spend significant amounts of money on legal counsel to prove that.

If you get your license, it raises your chances of being sued. Even if you are not at fault. When a project is not performing as designed, the first point of contact is always the architect who orchestrated the project. Without a license, you cannot be the Architect of Record. However, in America, anyone can sue anyone for anything, so you haven't truly avoided responsibility.

4. Avoid the extra work: IDP, ARE and never-ending continuing education.

I found the Intern Development Program (IDP) incredibly frustrating to figure out and a tedious chore to stay on top of. If there's anything to recognize about getting the architecture license, it's that it is a lot of work. After you're licensed, you have to complete continuing education requirements every year to maintain an active license; otherwise your state will take it away. All of this stuff is a lot of extra work. Especially if you're already working full-time at an architecture firm.

5. Avoid the never-ending fees.

You have already made a huge financial commitment by investing in architecture school. It was a great investment. I will be paying for my education for many more years to come.

Getting licensed sure was cheaper than going to grad school, but I also did sign myself up for a ridiculous amount of NCARB, AIA ,and state licensing fees to maintain my license. Joining the AIA is optional, although if you're using your membership appropriately, it should theoretically pay for itself. Nevertheless, NCARB and AIA membership costs about $1,000 every year after you're licensed.

6. Avoid the major time commitment.

I typically spent about 100 hours +/- to study for each architect registration exam.

      100 hours x 7 tests = 700 hours.

      Say you're normal and fail only two exams. Add on 200 more hours retaking.

Total = 900 hours of studying

A complete year of full-time work is about 2,000 hours. **Do you have 900 hours to squeeze in after you work a full-time job?**

One of my most frustrating moments was when I put down my ARE study book and realized that with all the time, money, and focused energy I already spent working through those exams, I could have built a profitable business from scratch, gotten another degree, or achieved some other worthy goal in life.

7. Your skills are better spent not being a Licensed Architect.

You may be best utilized by the profession and by society through having a skill which licensure has nothing to do with. Maybe you're a brilliant: construction (fill in the blank) expert, spec writer, marketing expert, project manager, model builder, renderer, CAD expert, or whatever.

Having an architecture license would be nice, but it will not help you further your personal goals or skills, whatever they may be. If that is the case, you should channel all the time, money, and energy into perfecting your craft to serve the greater good.

8. There are millions of great jobs you could do in other industries with your architecture training.

I have always believed that an education in architecture is one of the best educations anyone could receive. **Architecture teaches you to be a brilliant problem solver.** It touches upon so many skills, topics, and directions that anyone could run with in their lives. It"s naïve to think that working in an architecture firm and practicing architecture in a way that requires a license is the only direction that you could go with this training.

You could make more money and have a successful career without the architecture certification, working in a subset of the profession: marketing, graphic design, entrepreneurialism, real estate, construction, or something that hasn't even been invented yet. The possibilities are endless.

9. The architecture career is merely a stepping stone to something else.

I don't believe that the career of showing up at the same cubicle every day for 30 years or so and then "retiring"" will be the same for our generation as it was for our parents' generation.

The Internet has drastically changed the global economy. Today, a lot people are making a lot of money in ways that were unimaginable 10 years ago. I don't believe that **the future of the architecture firm will look and operate the same way it has for the past 100 years.**

After graduating architecture school and working for several years, you have learned that spending 40 hours a week working in the cubicle may not be how you want to spend the next 30 years. Maybe your dream is to escape your architecture office, take all the skills you learned from architecture, and apply your talents to building something else in another industry, realm, or dimension. You"re certainly qualified to do so.

10. Your loved ones will be affected by your decision to get licensed.

Maybe you have kids, a spouse, a family, or others that are dependent on how you spend your time. They will be affected by the time you commit and how you go about committing your time to the licensing process.

Like I said earlier, many people raise families and finish the licensing process, but it shouldn't be ignored that juggling life and the licensing process is definitely a challenge.

Don't let other people's stories affect yours.

I went to a job interview four years after I graduated, and I mentioned I was in the middle of my exams. The interviewer told me that it didn't look good that I hadn't already completed my AREs and that I was approaching that threshold of people who will never complete it.

I didn't get that job, and I walked out of there not even wanting it. Maybe he was right. I don't know or care. I do know that sooo many things had happened in my life between graduation and that job interview. Who was he to pass judgment on the pace at which I was completing the exams?? Finishing the exams in one year wasn't my story. Others may make you feel bad for not making the same decisions they made. That's their story and not yours.

I support you.

You could be healthier and happier and live a more fulfilling life if you do not go down the road of getting your architecture license. Only you know the answer to that. If that is that case, I fully support you in your decision.

During architecture school, I watched many people realize that being in the architecture program just wasn't for them. During that time, I watched their lives change course and saw them move toward other goals. Architecture brought them clarity as to where they wanted to go with their life. I commend them for figuring it out and changing direction.

I also watched several people push and force themselves through a degree they weren't passionate about or didn't really have any interest in. It was painful to watch, and it was painful to be their peer.

Not having your architecture license could be the best thing if your heart is not in it. There's nothing wrong with not wanting it.

My story isn't yours.

I mentioned earlier that I got my architecture license because I needed the closure. **I truly got my license because having it was crucial, considering where I wanted to take my career.** I actually used my architect stamp four times within the first year of having it.

I had very strong beliefs about why I felt I needed it, but if my beliefs hadn't been so strong, I would have wasted my time. Trust me, this thing is a lot of work, and your resources could be channeled into something that you are more passionate about. It's ok if you don't do this. If it's not really for you, then you will be better off in the long run.

Ten Good Reasons to Get Your Architecture License

If you've already read the previous chapter and are still thinking that becoming a Licensed Architect might be for you, here's a whole list of reasons to perk up, stay focused, and pass the ARE:

1. **Having an architectural license will not hurt your career.**
    Whether you use it or not doesn't matter. It's an accomplishment obtaining this credential, and it is acknowledged.

2. **It will make you a better architect.**
    Throughout the ARE process, you'll learn stuff you didn't learn in architecture school. In school, I learned a lot about design, architecture history, theory, art, and building construction. Taking the ARE forces you to read, retain, and be tested on material you never learned in college. The knowledge I gained studying for the ARE made me a better employee and a better architect.

3. **Studying for the ARE is more valuable than most people think.**
    It will re-teach you how to learn, especially in the subjects you don't want to study. It made me realize that if I channeled this much energy into making money, building a business, or building anything, I would be in a very different place. It"s really a test in discipline and following directions. It's a self-guided process, as opposed to the old-school way of testing in one day. This is the second-best lesson in work ethic and discipline I have ever gotten in my life. (Architecture school was the first.)

4. **You can finally call yourself an Architect.**
    Technically, it is illegal to call yourself an Architect and solicit architectural services (involving health safety and welfare of the public) without having an architectural license. Whether you view this as fortunate or unfortunate, this is regularly enforced by your state's architecture licensing board. And, as an added bonus, the interns now get to work for you! You can even sign off on others' IDP and finally start that intern development sweatshop that you have always been dreaming about. I'm just kidding.

5. **Make yourself credible**.
    Society respects credentials. Like it or not. People that don't know anything about

the profession care. Regardless of what career path you choose later on, being a Licensed Architect will provide you with more employment opportunities than staying uncertified.

6. **Anyone can pass this test.**
   It's not really a hard exam. It's just a lot of work. NCARB makes it hard and expensive to get to this point.

7. **You only have to do this once.**
   Everyone's thought to themselves prior to doing something they couldn't figure out a way of avoiding, ""This is one day of my life. Then it's over." Like becoming a tenured professor, no one can take your certification away from you unless you do something really, really bad.

8. **You have five years to git 'er done.**
   Think back to what was going on in your life five years ago. Doesn't it seem like a long time has passed? Five years gives you a really long window to complete seven exams. I even took a two-year break in the middle of my exams, which I would not recommend. A conservative estimate for me was that I needed three months to prepare for each test, while working full-time.

9. **The study materials have gotten better since I started.**
   There are really great resources available now that I wish I had access to when I was taking the exam. Ballast and Kaplan were really the only names I had to help me study.

10. **You have already paid a premium to be eligible to take this exam.**
    Why waste the time and money you've already paid when there are so many benefits to studying for and passing the ARE?

Visualize the Possibilities

Hopefully, after reading the previous two chapters, you have pondered the many valid reasons for and against taking the exam. If you have decided to get your license, having a clear understanding of why you are taking the ARE is fundamental to success. Even if you already know deep down in your heart why you are taking it, visualizing it is completely different.

By visualizing it, you create visual associations. Even though visualizations aren't real, the mind doesn't always know the difference. Often what you visualize in the present manifests as the reality of the future.

The interesting thing about the human mind is that it is extremely malleable. Something does not have to be real for the brain to believe it. I don't want to point any fingers, but there're definitely some people who speak with very strong conviction about stuff we know isn"t real. The interesting thing is that whatever three-headed alien they worship actually is real on some level.

It's real to them.

Were you ever the kid that told another kid who really believed in Santa that he's not real? This revelation can send some children into shock. If you're told that something is a certain way enough times, you start to visualize it. ""Visions of sugar plums danced in their heads." Then you start to believe what you visualize, even if you know the first time you hear it—on a cognitive level—that what you're being expected to believe is completely outrageous.

If you can convince a child that someone with magical powers is real through visualization, imagine how you could channel that into something authentically possible — like passing an exam.

I recommend that you do a visualization exercise. When I do these exercises, I usually spend a lot of time writing this stuff out in explicit detail. I consider all aspects of my personal, professional and social life. Then after I'm done, I rip the whole thing up. Knowing that what I am writing will be destroyed sometimes allows me to really open up and be completely transparent with what I am thinking.

Or, you could keep a copy of your writing tucked away for later—it may come in handy if you need to validate your decision or require some additional motivation.

Part 1

I recommend you spend at least 30 minutes writing this out. There is no right or wrong way of doing this. However, it is critical you add as much detail as possible to your visions. Don't forget to consider ALL aspects of your life—not just your career!

1. How will having my architecture license change this immediate moment in your life? That means right now, your current job and personal situation.

2. What will be different in one year after you have this license? What kind of projects will you be working on, and what is your role? What type of family or personal responsibilities will you have?

3. What does your architecture practice look like in five years? How have you grown? What does your personal or family life look like in five years? Are you married? How old will your kids be?

4. In 15 years?

5. Come back to the present moment. What will studying and passing these exams look like over the next six months? One year? What personal and family sacrifices will you have to make?

Part 2

Do it for the opposite, but I only want you to spend 15 minutes in this area.

1. How will **not** having my architecture license change the immediate moment in your life? Right now, your current job and personal situation.

2. What will be different in one year if you **don't have this license?** What kind of project will you be working on, and what is your role? What type of family and personal responsibilities will you have?

3. In five years?

4. In 15 years?

5. What have you gained by **not investing in and not studying** for these exams? Have you realized any personal or professional benefit?

Although it might feel a little strange, this visualization exercise will help solidify your decision to proceed with the exams and give you the momentum you need to get started. If you get stuck at any time during the licensing process, I recommend repeating this exercise, especially during any setbacks you encounter during the exam. If you get stuck, visualizing the future may just give you the jumpstart you need.

By spending 45 minutes visualizing your future, you are guaranteed to gain a better understanding of what you are gaining and what you are giving up—in the short run and in the long run.

Part 3
The Mental

Mentally Preparing for the Exam

The Mental Shift

At the beginning of my architecture licensing process, I followed the normal steps. Finish IDP, get approval to start testing, pass a few exams. Then I got frustrated and got stuck in the middle of it.

I wasn't ready.

I had been living in the architecture student/intern world for too long. To me, architecture was a job.

I was mad and frustrated about when I arrived in the architecture industry. During the recession of 2009, there was very little opportunity for architects because no one was building anything. At that time, my goals were to support myself and to not **have** to move into my parents' basement in my late 20s. Paying NCARB fees, buying study materials, and giving all my free time to study for an exam just didn't make sense at that time.

I needed to live my life. There is more to life than architecture. In fact, there's a lot more. After my lengthy education, I needed to live the life of a normal person, hang out with my friends, and get into hobbies that had nothing to do with architecture.

After several years…

I was ready.

I stopped being an intern and became an architect. This happened one year prior to passing the remaining exams and getting the license.

I had decided that nothing was going to get in the way. I was finishing the exams no matter what.

I started having a lot more respect for the profession. I felt like the process of working on the exams helped me gain the confidence to be a better architect and start taking on a lot more responsibility.

Mental shift

After I made this mental shift, everything changed. Finishing my exams almost became inevitable; it was happening no matter what.

Studying actually made me realize that I truly love working hard. Sure, I don't miss taking tests, but honestly, after I was done studying, I took all that momentum and immediately transitioned it into working on projects, creating a blog, and building my own architecture practice.

The most important thing was that for me, the mental shift of being a Licensed Architect happened long before finishing the exams. I stopped being an intern and mentally started seeing myself as an architect, and I just needed the license to make it official.

It's normal to get frustrated or sidetracked at some point during the ARE process. Life happens, after all. But, when you are truly ready to complete the exams, you will know it.

You may not necessarily experience an architectural epiphany, but embracing the process and respecting the craft—even when things get tough—will help you maintain the momentum you need to achieve your goal.

Commit to Showing Up

Architecture is one of the most competitive professions. It starts the second you apply to design school, and it never stops. Hustling is rewarded more than talent. Showing up is frequently 75 percent of the battle.

People who are half as talented as you will typically work three times as hard just to raise the standard. They will be rewarded, get their buildings built, and frequently outperform you.

And just like the architecture profession, passing the ARE is directly correlated to the ability to show up and study and put in the work. Talent, smarts, money, and experience are not shortcuts to showing up and consistently working on this exam.

Just like architecture school, I believe everyone will have a moment in the process that will be really easy for them. I also believe there will be an opposite moment when everyone is pushed really hard.

Showing up—no matter what—is the hardest part.

It actually took me twice as much time to study for the exams than I thought it would when I started. As it turned out, allotting time to study typically came from my weekends, weeknights after work, lunch breaks, and even waking up at 5 a.m. to study for a little bit before I went into the office.

The funny thing is that after I committed to showing up, the studying wasn't that hard. I really felt like showing up every day was significantly more difficult than actually studying the material.

What I am trying to say is there is no shortcut in taking the ARE. I think there will be a moment when your experience helps you, but those moments are few and far between. Don't think you don't have to work at passing because you have a lot of experience in a certain portion of the exam.

The ability to show up—day after day, week after week, and exam after exam—is a shortcut.

Before you embark on the AREs, I recommend that you do what you can to organize your life so you can devote your free time and attention to the test. And, prepare yourself for a bumpy ride at times. By anticipating the amount work that you will need to put in and the difficulty of the exam up front, you will be better equipped to continue showing up when the going gets tough.

Be Prepared to Sacrifice

Good goals aren't easy to achieve. You cannot achieve any goal unless you sacrifice something.

I sacrificed a lot just to go to architecture school:

- I took out an incredible amount of student loans.
- I had very little social life.
- I gave years of my life to the process.

I also milked it for all it was worth, and all those sacrifices were very much worth what I got from being in architecture school.

I sacrificed a lot to finish my exams:

- I sacrificed my wallet and I happily paid fees, bought study materials, and ate out because I didn't have time to cook. Money was not going to stop me from being successful on my exams.
- I gave all of my free time to the ARE.
- I sacrificed anything that was not moving me toward completing the ARE, including socializing, hobbies, watching movies, reading books, and even getting drunk with my friends. It was all sacrificed so I could finish my exams.

I went into this mode several times for weeks at a time. But if I added up all this time together, it would have amounted to close to two years.

It isn't entirely healthy, and I'm not recommending it. But it is what I did. I felt like my entire life was on hold until I finished the ARE.

Sacrificing can accelerate success.

I became extremely discouraged when I failed the Structures exam the first time I took it. For round two, I decided to use all-new study material. I realized that time was my most valuable resource. I needed to do whatever I could to use it more effectively. I stopped wasting time, and I stopped worrying about the financial impact the exams were having on my life. I made big cuts everywhere else to make that happen.

After a lot of debate, I dropped $400 and signed up for Mark Mitalski's PrepARE course. The course consists of 36 hours of online video of Mark teaching structures in a way that directly addresses the content of the exam outlined by NCARB. I really enjoyed this class. I feel like it quickly got me up and running by presenting the material in a logical order that builds upon itself. He also brought a lot of personal information and stories to the class, which really helped me tie it all together.

Throwing money at the exam was part of the sacrifice. Once I realized that, I made peace with spending money that I didn't really have on a structures class, and I made sure I sucked all the value out of it.

Shortly before I retook the exam, I reviewed Ballast and Kaplan again from round one, and I got a lot more out of that information. I killed it the second time, and now it's over. Passing the Structures test was my proudest moment of 2013.

It's about choices.

If you say yes to the exams, **you MUST say no to something else.** It's your decision to decide what that is. Unless you are willing to sacrifice something, becoming a Licensed Architect is not going to happen.

Seek Others Out.

You are not alone. Luckily there are many, many, many other people taking the ARE. When I was taking the exams, I must have met, talked to, or knew of about 30-40 people who either didn't get very far at all or gave up halfway through.

I really only knew 3 or 4 people who tested and completed the process at the same time I did. Nevertheless, it was always really helpful for me to connect with those people while I went through the process.

When I was testing, the ARE Forum existed, and it was kind of a cold, lonely place to discuss the exam. People were often rude, or the people just beginning a new division would repeatedly ask the same questions that 1,000 other people just asked. There was lots of great content and discussions on there, but the problem was finding it was like finding a needle in a haystack.

My experiences at the ARE Forum helped inspire me to start writing the Young Architect blog.

NCARB and the exams are changing and moving in a positive direction, in my opinion. I don't think the process will be as lonely in the future as it was for me.

Here are some ideas about working with other people. Just keep in mind when you discuss the exams to respect NCARB's privacy policy.

Do it as a group.

I know someone who had a tight-knit group of friends from grad school, and they went through the process together. They met regularly to discuss the exams, and I think they even took them together as a group.

Connect with people online.

At the time of this writing, NCARB had just started their Google+ group. There is also an excellent group of people on Facebook, discussing the exams and sharing helpful studying tricks. There are links to both on **YoungArchitect.com/AREBook.**

Find people locally.

I met people at the AIA ARE Classes and connected with them after class. I had a few friends, and we would have coffee and talk about the exam process. That was really helpful.

Set up an accountability partner.

I check in weekly with a friend of mine to discuss everything going on. I have been doing this for a few months now. My friend is in a completely different profession. We talk to each other for 30 minutes once a week. We each take 15 minutes. Here's the drill:

> Talk about the successes of the past week.
>
> Talk about the struggles or issues, and discuss solutions.
>
> Talk about what is going to be accomplished in the next week.

While each person is talking, the other person writes down what they say and then asks them about it during the next week's call. I wish I'd had this friend and was doing this when I was studying for the exams.

Surround yourself with like-minded people.

I encourage you to find and surround yourself with other people that are taking the ARE or people who are not in architecture but are working very hard towards a goal that is similar to yours. I have learned that it can sometimes be hard to connect with people who are in a different place than you are. Specifically, it can be challenging to connect with people that aren't working towards a goal.

The self-guided process is one of the biggest challenges when taking the ARE.

Understand How You Learn

The self-guided process of studying for the ARE is drastically different than what studying was like for lecture-style classes in architecture school. It is absolutely critical to figure out how you learn so you can study efficiently and effectively. And, the sooner you can figure this out, the better off you will be.

After a significant amount of trial and error and constantly reevaluating my process, I figured out a few things about my learning style that helped me get through the Architecture Registration Exam. Here's what worked for me:

Step 1: I need to care. If I don't care, then I need to brainwash myself into genuinely caring about the material. Treat it as if it's the most important, exciting information in the world. I used to constantly remind myself that taking these exams was making me a better architect, a better person, and a contributor to the greater good. I would ask myself, "Why are you doing this? Why do you care?"

Step 2: When reading material that is highly technical or dry (ahem, Ballast), I need to **mark up, highlight, underline whatever it is I'm trying to extract** from that information. Basically, strip away all the extra words.

Step 3: I need to **rewrite the information in my own words** and make them my own. Kaplan sometimes has an awkward way of saying things, using more words than necessary.

Step 4: This is the most important step. I need to **genuinely think about what I'm reading.** I would try to think about it in a context outside of the book. I'd consider what the application in real life would be.

Step 5: Keep revisiting it and thinking about. Instead of only reading the material once and expecting to absorb it, I'd multiply the frequency I"d think about that topic.

That is my formula for learning. I apply it often, especially when I feel I have better things to do. I guarantee that your learning process is different than mine. But, my goal is to get you thinking about what might work for you.

As you move through the process, pay close attention to how you learn and what methods of studying are helpful to you. And, remember to be flexible—you might find that you need to adjust your study methods depending on your mood, your study environment, or the exam.

Focus on Yourself… Not Others

Comparing yourself to others who have completed the exam is a lesson I have learned does not work.

You might find yourself saying something like,

> "Michael Riscica completed the exams, and I am a lot smarter than him in many ways. So, the ARE can't be that much work, and I shouldn't have to study that hard.""

Even if you are correct (and you probably are), I don't agree with that logic. Skill, talent, life experience and smarts certainly help in the process, but as we've discussed in previous sections, this test is really about showing up, focusing on what you are studying, and passing an exam.

Everyone is on their own self-guided journey with the ARE, and it's really about being a good test taker. Which I was not. Which I learned to be.

NCARB wants you to think taking these exams is no big deal, and you can do it in one year. But the reality is it takes most people several years to complete the exams.

If you compare yourself to others' results, you're going to stress yourself out in a way that won't be helpful to you when taking the test. If Don Jones passed the test in less than a year, good for him. He's an expedient genius in test-taking.

Some people have a natural aptitude for passing exams. Does that mean that you're not going to be a good (or even extraordinary) architect if you aren't able to pass the ARE as quickly as Don Jones? Of course not.

What is your goal with taking the ARE? Is it to take the test in less time than Don Jones, even if it means failing due to lack of preparation and accumulating a small fortune in retest fees? Or is it because you truly want to be a certified architect?

If your true goal is the latter, don't let yourself get caught up in competition or comparison. This will only be detrimental and counterproductive to you in the long-term.

Passing the ARE means becoming a good test taker for you as an individual. It has nothing to do with comparing yourself to someone else. Don Jones' tactics might work extremely well for him, but they might not work for you at all. It's vital to learn what works for you and develop your own timetable that makes sense to you, even if you encounter peer pressure to the contrary.

Part 4
The Studying

The Momentum Concept

Momentum with the ARE is very real.

Remember in architecture school when you struggled with finding a design solution? By showing up at the drafting table over and over again, the answers start to appear.

Frequently in my architecture school, there were people in my architecture school who would keep working on their projects for another week or two after final crit. Why??? Because it was hard for them to stop.

Imagine having a hard time stopping when studying for the ARE because you are in such a groove.

Starting to Build Momentum

The more I study, the easier it gets. The easier the studying gets, the easier it is to show up every day. This is how momentum is built. The more momentum you have, the easier it is to knock down barriers.

Starting to build momentum is the hardest part. It's like starting to run a marathon waist deep in mud. Nevertheless, running through the mud is actually making you stronger.

When I was studying, I would often postpone any information that I was intimidated by until I had already built substantial momentum with it. This made it easier to grasp the concept.

My momentum was extremely hard to build and incredibly easy to lose. But once I had it, I was on fire.

Studying for the architect exam isn't easy.

On my final push (after a two-year break), I tested four times in less than a year. The results: Three passes and one fail. I got into an aggressive competition with myself, trying to get these bastard exams out of my life.

When one test finished, I took about a week off from studying and then started working on the next one. At the end of 2013, I had such incredible momentum from those exams I never really stopped working. Except now I was working on what I really wanted to do.

I went on to build **YoungArchitect.com** and started looking for opportunities to use my Architect stamp.

Someone recently asked me how I built such strong momentum. It took me a few minutes to realize it, but this is what I did.

I studied every day

At one point I decided I needed to study every single day. Easier said than done, but it actually wasn't that hard. In reality, you actually can't study every single day. You'll fry your brain and go insane.

On days when I was mentally exhausted, or when I was first starting out, I would make it super easy and just spend about 20 minutes reading something light. Maybe something from a past exam that will be applicable to this one, or even reading the forums. Small moves, but lots of them.

Finding the hidden little tasks of studying for the ARE (small moves)

When I started testing, I realized that there are a lot of little small tasks that need to take place that have nothing to do with actual studying. These may look like:

- Scheduling a test date.
- Installing the vignette software.
- Locating which study materials I needed for each exam.
- Printing study guides or information from the web.
- Uploading vignettes to the forums and reviewing other candidates' vignettes.
- Going to the office supply store to buy index cards so I could make my own flashcards.
- Selling study material from exams I had already passed.
- Reorganizing my calendar so I could work full-time and still have long study sessions on the weekends.

All these little things add up.

Finding the light and easy stuff (more small moves)

I worked 40 hours a week while I took all seven tests. Often after a hectic workday, the thought of reading anything technical would make me feel sick to my stomach. When this happened I would:

- Read something light and easy related to the exam.
- Watch YouTube videos.
- Look at other people's vignettes.
- Call up my study partners and see how they were doing.
- Briefly scan over all the chapters in the book before I actually read them.

On these days, maybe I only had the mental bandwidth to do this for 5-10 minutes, but it almost didn't matter as long as I was still making small moves with studying every day. A few days later, when I had the mental capacity to get into the study material, the small moves I had previously made set me up for success.

On the weekends, I would always make an effort to get a few hours in and make a big move

What does a big move look like?

- Digesting massive amounts of information.
- Learning how to do the vignettes.
- Spending long, extended amounts of time focusing on the exam.

You are better off studying for 20 minutes three or four days in a row than studying once every four days for an hour and a half. Building the habit of studying is one of the hardest things with this exam.

Once you have that habit, the material you need to know to pass these exams is actually pretty interesting. I constantly told myself:

"Studying for these exams is making me a better architect."

And it's true.

I also told everyone:

"I study for the Architect's exam every single day."

With a "Look at me. I am so cool" attitude. But by saying it over and over again, it also helped the habit of studying every day stick.

The Studying Every Single Day Rules

1. Avoid completely stopping your studying for the exam by making small moves as you have to, until you can make big moves.

2. Constantly remind yourself (and everyone else) that you study every day by talking about it.

3. If you miss a day, you're not allowed to beat yourself up. Just make up for it the next day. No big deal.

Don't flip the off switch on your studying, if you can avoid it. Be an object in motion, and stay in motion.

I wrote a guest blogpost about this on NCARB's blog. For a link to that article, visit my Resources page at **YounArchitect.com/AREbook.**

I tracked my study time.

I tracked all the hours I spent studying, similar to how I'd track my time on projects in the office or IDP. I only logged hours I was physically studying. Walking to Starbucks, printing things out, or shopping for materials didn't count.

Having these numbers really helped me gauge how hard I was studying. When I started studying for an exam, I did about 3-4 hours a week. Toward the end when I was in the final push, I was doing about 10-14 hours a week.

It's easy to think that you're studying a lot, when in reality you're not, and vice versa. Time is deceiving, especially when you're doing something you don't want to do.

I thought of studying as a marathon, not a sprint.

Just studying harder isn't always better.

Running a marathon and studying for the ARE exam have a lot in common.

- Burnout is frequent.

- They both involve many long hours of unglamorous work.

- Many people do not meet their goals or finish.

- Both involve many small victories, working toward the big one.

- Slow and steady usually finishes the race.

I actually ran two marathons in 2010 and learned a lot about myself in the process.

I worked out a lot.

Halfway through training for my first marathon, I decided one day to try my first yoga class. I was frustrated with running and thought it could help my stiff legs. I walked in with a "what the hell, why not" attitude.

Little did I know that yoga almost immediately changed everything about running for me. It stretched out my legs and opened my hips more than they ever had been. This allowed me to get past the 18-mile threshold I kept hitting with my runs. Yoga quickly became my secret weapon with my marathon training.

Take care of yourself.

During that final push, I pretty much went to yoga 4-5 times a week and ate a very clean diet. I got into the best shape of my life. Between working out and studying as hard as I could, I was so exhausted there wasn't much room for anything else in my life.

I also go to a yoga studio that brings a lot of self-actualization and personal development into their practice. This helped put me in a good mindset for studying. The yoga also allowed me to escape, and I didn't think about anything else while I was there.

Sure, I know yoga isn't for everyone, but working out and moving my body really helped my mind concentrate.

When I was studying, there were a few things that I did when I needed to take a break from the massive amounts of reading text. None of which involve doing yoga, although that will also help if that's your thing.

Go to the AIA classes.

My AIA offers ARE classes that last about two hours, and they mostly just review the practice questions from the NCARB study guides. I went to a lot of these, even the classes for exams I had already passed.

It was good to get a refresher about stuff I already studied, because you do see a lot of the same stuff on subsequent exams. Sometimes I could also offer some insight to someone else studying for an exam I had already taken.

Use the practice exams to study, rather than practice.

When I needed a break from information intake, I would study the practice exams. I would typically answer two or three questions at time, and then look up the answers in the back of the book. This allowed me to quickly correct myself if I got the answer wrong, rather than waiting until I finished the exam. They are also a great way of getting into the rhythm of answering questions just like they are on the test.

I worked the practice exams mostly during my lunch break. They are also easier to carry around then that awful Ballast book that weighs 10 pounds. Practice exams brought me much sanity. Check out my recommended list of study materials **on YoungArchitect.com/AREbook** for links to practice exams for each exam.

Momentum was a really powerful tool for me. As I have said many times throughout this book—the exact methods that worked for me will probably not work for you. So, pay close attention to what drives you. If you recognize, respect and commit to maintaining your momentum, you"ll be much more likely to bounce back quickly from inevitable setbacks and stay on track.

Creating Good Energy

One of the concepts I played with during the exam was creating a really good energy around myself, especially with everything that had to do with the exams.

I am not a religious person, but I generally believe that "like attracts like".

When you're a happy positive person that is actively contributing to society and spreading good energy, you will attract similar people and situations into your life.

Or

When you're a pissed off jerk that has no patience, you will tend to encounter a lot of other grumpy people and negative situations.

While I was studying, I was also working 40 hours a week. I was under an incredible amount of stress from the exams and my job and pushing myself really hard.

During this time, I did everything I could to create a good energy around myself.

I worked out a lot and made it a priority.

By being active, it really helped burn off a lot of stress and mental steam, which significantly helped with studying longer and harder. I have learned that after I exercise, it boosts my endorphins, leaving me feeling good and at peace with the world. My ability to concentrate gets significantly boosted.

Experiment with exercising before you study, and see if it helps your ability focus and read boring textbooks.

However, this is something that you should ease your way into, rather than jumping into it head first. If exercise isn't a part of your normal routine, then your first goal should be on consistency and building the habit more than anything else.

I ate really healthy.

I paid a lot of attention to what I was putting into my body and how that impacted my studying. When I ate a clean diet that included foods like veggies, chicken, salad, and fruit, I felt much more present and capable of sitting and doing the work.

When I ingested rice, bread, sugary junk food, beef, potatoes, or alcohol, it left me feeling tired and often resulted in unproductive studying or no studying at all.

I donated money to charities.

On and off for the past few years, I have been putting a portion of my paycheck aside for charity. Since the money is already set aside, it is available to use when an opportunity to do some good presents itself. I used this money to help friends and other people in need and support charities. During the exams, I consistently donated, and I even upped the percentage I was contributing.

I volunteered my time.

During the exams, my time was my most valuable resource. I didn't have a lot of it.

For years, I had been saying I was going to volunteer for the Architects in Schools program that teaches grade school kids about architecture. But I always told them I was too busy.

In 2013, when they made their annual request, my first response was, **"Yeah right, I'm too busy. I am trying to finish the ARE this year."** But then it occurred to me that I'd been saying that same thing for several years prior, so I just signed up. The year I started volunteering right in the middle of my exams, I was actually busier than every other year I claimed I was too busy.

Working with the kids actually became a wonderful outlet for me to disengage from studying. Sure, it added another thing onto my already full plate, but I definitely think the volunteering actually indirectly helped me pass. Committing some of my free time forced me to be more focused and effective with the time I did have to study.

I also had just as much fun as the kids did during our time together.

I tried to live a clean life.

During the exams, I basically stopped kicking cats, drowning puppies, and stealing eBooks from people trying to help me. I didn't want any kind of bad karma coming around when I took those exams. I'm just kidding about the cats and puppies, but I really didn't do anything that jeopardized my good energy. No drama. I didn't want anything trivial getting in the way.

As you prepare for the exam, you might want to see if there is any "housekeeping" that needs to be done in other areas of your life. Creating good energy, taking care of yourself, and committing to living healthfully will put you in the best possible position to tackle the ARE.

Choosing A Testing Order

Everyone wants to know, **"What's the best testing order for the Architect Registration Exam?"**

Having seven exams to tackle in five years, many people spend a lot of time worrying about the best order to take the ARE. Where the hell do you even get started?

CDS, PPP, SPD, SD, SS, BS, BDCS

That's what I did.

That order, or a variation of it, is what many people do.

Before I give you all the details, there is something very important that you need to know.

You will get questions from any exam on any exam.

At the beginning of the process, you are at a disadvantage because you have zero AREs under your belt.

At the end of the process, you are at a disadvantage because you have forgotten everything you memorized from the first few exams.

To answer your question about which test to take first:

It doesn't matter.

Do what works for you.

If you kick ass at structures, go right ahead and take that first. Or if you want to conquer the vignettes early, then take SD First. You really just need to pick the exam that you happen to have the most advantage with, and start there.

Everyone who has taken these tests will have a different experience with the AREs. You should **tailor your journey to whatever works best for you.** Start with whatever you feel comfortable starting with.

Worrying about the testing order is a spot where a lot of people get stuck (and spend too much time worrying about) before they actually start working. Which test you take first is much less important than getting started. Just start studying.

If you're still concerned about the order, here're some things to consider:

The CDS, PPP, and SPD Trifecta

Many people like to take CDS, PPP, and SPD in that order because the study materials build upon each other. Here's why…

Construction Documents and Services (CDS)

The CDS contains tons of legal contract stuff, the basics of Architecture as a business, and a glimpse at some of the basics of working in an architecture office or creating construction drawings. Having no testing experience, this test is usually the one that most ARE Candidates are least intimidated by and have an existing practical knowledge of.

Programming, Planning, and Practice (PPP)

A great deal of what was studied in CDS will directly carry over into PPP. PPP gets into the early stages of a project, and it looks at programming and early design concepts.

Site Planning and Design (SPD)

Since site planning is integral to the early stages of the design process, this is where the broad design concepts learned in PPP start considering the site. I personally found the SPD vignettes to be tricky to get the hang of, but having CDS and PPP under my belt helped.

As a disclaimer, I must say that many people, but not everyone, follow the philosophy of this trifecta.

The Island Exams (SD, SS)

I call these exams islands because the content doesn't really have any distinctly overlapping information. Depending upon how comfortable you are with these subjects, these exams could be very challenging or an easy win.

Schematic Design (SD)

This is about solving two graphic vignettes. You may want to consider how comfortable you are with the NCARB software as a gauge to taking this test sooner or later.

Structural Systems (SS)

I have never been great with calculations and all the little nuances of structures. I could see how this test could be a walk in the park for some other people. There is a bit of an overlap with BDCS either way.

BS and BDCS aren't BS

I thought there was some overlap in the content I studied for BS and BDCS. There are really BDCS questions on all the exams.

Building Systems (BS)

During architecture school, I had a professor who would yell about how the knowledge he is teaching us in his building systems class would make us more money than any other subjects being taught. His basis was that the better educated architects were in these subjects, the less they would have to rely on engineers to do it all for them. Nevertheless, the BS test is all about Mechanical, Electrical, Plumbing, HVAC, Acoustics, Elevators, etc.

For a more detailed description of what is included on each test, you can refer to the study guides that I link to on **YoungArchitect.com/AREbook**.

Consider ARE 5.0

NCARB recently announced that with the rollout of ARE 5.0, it is important to get CDS, PPP, and SPD taken care of before the transition goes into effect. Maybe that is something you should take into consideration.

In June 2018, ARE 4.0 will be retired, and the clock has already started ticking to get in and get out.

The most important thing to consider.

At the end of the day, **it doesn't really matter** which test you take first. I have watched many people burn a ton of energy worrying about this, and they never actually begin the process.

What really matters is…   **Are you REALLY going to show up to study over and over again and do all this hard work?**

What really matters is…   **When you fail an exam, are you going to let it deflate your dreams of becoming a Licensed Architect?**

If you could just get those two mindsets taken care of, you're three-quarters of the way there.

Stop planning, and just start studying.

Create a Study Schedule

Since I worked a full-time job and paid all of my own bills, it took me approximately 90 days to prepare for each exam. For my last four exams, I kept records of how much time I spent legitimately studying. This came out to approximately 100 hours per exam.

Scheduling the test would always fall around the middle of the process. I would typically study for a period of time until I felt like I had my head around the entire test. Then I would schedule the exam and spend as much time getting a much better understanding of the material. When following the sample schedule below, I recommend scheduling the test on day 45 of my 90-day studying fest.

Scheduling the test was always an important milestone for me. The minute I had a test date, my mindset and attitude about the exam would immediately change.

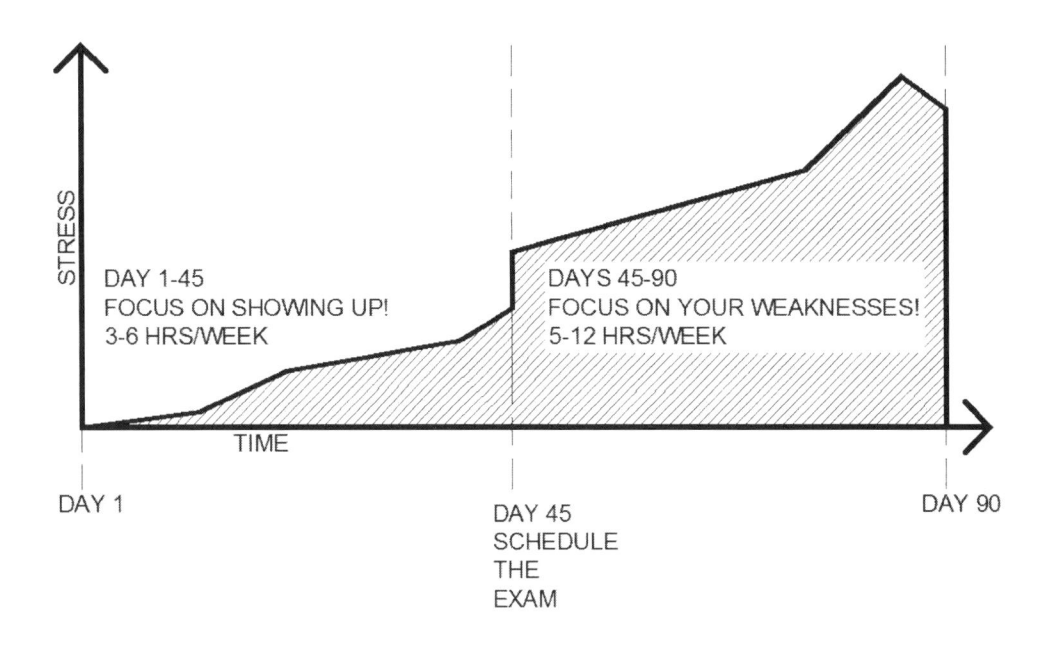

STRESS vs TIME

DAY 1-45
FOCUS ON SHOWING UP!
3-6 HRS/WEEK

DAYS 45-90
FOCUS ON YOUR WEAKNESSES!
5-12 HRS/WEEK

DAY 1 | DAY 45 SCHEDULE THE EXAM | DAY 90

Before I had a test date, I focused more on showing up and getting through the material. My studying was more relaxed. I wouldn't worry so much if I didn't quite get it. My goals were to get a feel for the entire exam and to figure out what I already knew and still needed to learn. During this period of time, I would typically study 3-6 hours a week.

After I had a test date, I focused all my energy on what I wasn't good at. I focused on filling in all the gaps. It was more important to me to get the practice questions wrong and then correct them. I felt like I was wasting my time reading stuff that I already knew. During this period of time, I would typically study 5-14 hours a week.

Sample ARE Studying Schedule

Day 0—First exam? Just pick one.

If this is your first exam, just start somewhere. I would recommend printing out all the NCARB Exam Guides and working on all the sample questions to get a taste for what is on each exam. I"ve included links to the guides at **YoungArchitect.com/AREbook**. As discussed in the previous chapter, there are all types of theories about testing order, but spending too much time worrying about it is silly because you'll have to take them all anyway.

If you don't already own it, I highly recommend you purchase *The Architecture Registration Exam Review Manual* **by David Kent Ballast.** Skim through the entire Ballast book and pick an exam to start on.

Day 1—Look at a calendar.

> **Million dollar ARE question:** Do you even have the time to spend the next three months studying your ass off?

What is going on in your life for the next three months? Brother's wedding? Birthday parties? Babies being born? Bachelor parties? Bar mitzvahs? Big vacations? Busy with out of town guests? Or even an epic rock concert that will leave you with a one-week hangover?

What's going on in the office? Traveling for business? Difficult, time-consuming clients? Project deadlines? Overtime? Boss is out of town and you have to hold down the fort?

It's best to try and attempt to identify these things ahead of time. If you need some guidance, I suggest re-reading the "Mental" section of this book.

I will guarantee you that some unforeseeable situation in your life will present itself to derail your studying.

That's ok.

Now that you know it's going to happen, you can expect it and plan for it.

Day 2—Start gathering studying materials. Buy, download, and get stuff printed out.

Getting started and building momentum was the hardest part for me. Gathering studying materials and doing basic exam research is pretty easy to do. I used this time to kick-start the process and set myself up for success over the next few weeks.

Figure out what materials you are going to use and buy them.

Download everything from the FTP site, Internet, and Jenny's Notes. Print out everything now to avoid having to do it later when you're busy studying.

March down to the office supply store, and buy a brick of index cards so you can make your own flashcards.

I've written several blog posts about the array of ARE study materials that are available. The links to the blog posts, as well as links to NCARB study guides and many other resources, can be found on my resources page at **YoungArchitect.com/AREbook**.

Day 2—Start making a first pass through study material A.

Find a study guide specifically written for the ARE that covers all areas of the exam you are studying for. Maybe its Kaplan, Ballast, or Architect Exam Prep. No, Jenny's Notes do not count. They are just notes and do not count as actually reading the book. You will use them later.

Start reading.

Focus on getting through all the content. In the first pass, it's more about getting a feel for the material than having a complete working knowledge of it.

Pay attention to **what you enjoy reading about**, **what you already know**, **what is painful to read,** or **what you have been trying to avoid**. This information is key for figuring out where you will need to supplement and channel more energy later.

Day 3—Start making flashcards for everything you don't know.

In the first pass, I made flashcards for all the vocabulary that I did not already know. Make flashcards for any information that you will need to remember. I never used a notebook and simply wrote things on flashcards.**Day 7—Start the vignette right away.**

I always worked on vignettes at the beginning. Some vignettes are harder than others, so I wanted to find out ASAP which ones those were.

I worked on the vignettes until I figured them out at a comfortable level. Then I took a break from them and revisited them a few weeks later.

At the beginning, I would study the program and then look at the solution, trying to draw the solution while looking at it. I would read the forums and look at other people's solutions. Work the vignettes until you feel about 75 percent comfortable with them, and come back to them later.

Day 21—Finish the first pass with study material A. Then start the first pass with study material B.

After you finish study material A, find another ARE study guide from a different author or publisher, and start making a first pass at study material B.

You always need to cross-train with different materials, especially on the topics that you find challenging. They each emphasize different topics, and some of the authors will resonate with you more than others.

Day 21—Start practice exams, and don't stop.

After you finished study material A and have had your first taste of the entire exam, you can now start using practice exams to test your ability to recall information. When working on practice exams, work on three questions at a time, and then go look up the answers. This method makes it easier to make the correction of information in your brain, rather than looking at the entire practice test.

Practice exams are also awesome for getting some productive studying done in short increments of time. I used to work on practice exams during my lunch break for 30-45 minutes at a time, and it was extremely efficient studying.

Day 44—Finish study material B.

Now you've studied two different ARE study materials. See how different they are.

Day 45—Go back to the calendar.

It's time to reevaluate. Spend some time thinking about the past and the future:

- How did this first 45 days go?
- Were you able to show up? How's your momentum? Can you keep showing up?
- What kinds of challenges came up during your studying? How did you handle them?
- Do you have an idea of what you need to focus on or where you need to be?
- Does your calendar look any different than it did 45 days ago?
- Are you ready to do this? What needs to happen?

Everything you need to do the work and pass the test is already inside of you. From here on out, it's more about focusing and showing up.

Day 45—Schedule the test.

Pick a date and schedule the test. Choose whatever works for you. I tended to prefer morning exams.

Day 46—Make a plan, and change your focus and attitude.

Plan out the remaining weeks until the exam.

I made a written plan of what I needed to spend more time working on and what I felt pretty comfortable with. This information would then guide how I channeled my time over the next few weeks.

If showing up to study is no longer the challenge, I recommend slowly starting to ramp up the length of the study sessions.

At this point in the game, I would start channeling all my energy into wherever my weaknesses were in the content. From this point on, it's a waste of valuable time studying stuff you already know, even though it's easy and strokes your ego for being so smart.

This is actually the opposite thinking from architecture school. During college, I typically downplayed (or avoided) things I wasn't good at and then overcompensated with the skills and areas that I was awesome at. I hated my technical structures classes and loved design class. I was terrible with 3-D computer modeling, but very comfortable with hand drafting and real model building. This was evident in all of my work. This approach worked really well for me in college, but it will not help with the ARE.

Don't get sucked into the trap of only studying material that is easy and makes you feel comfortable. A lot of people make this mistake. I definitely made this mistake at the beginning.

Start getting used to spending time studying stuff that makes you uncomfortable.

Day 46—Start working with study material C.

Add more supplementary study material in whatever topics you need more help with. This could be articles from the Internet, the FTP site, or even YouTube videos. If you need some ideas about new materials to try, check out my blog post on "The ULTIMATE list of NCARB ARE study material (Part 2)." I've included the link on my resource page at **YoungArchitect.com/AREbook**.

Day 48—Audit the flashcards. Get rid of the ones you know.

By this point, you should have a growing pile of flashcards. From the deck, start removing the cards you feel really comfortable with. Hang onto these for later. Keep adding more cards around the areas you are trying to improve in.

Keep flashcards everywhere, and keep using them every day.

Day 60—Revisit study materials A and B.

A lot has happened since you first reviewed this study material. You're smarter and in better studying shape. Plus, you've picked up more momentum. Now you"re in the thick of it.

Find everything that didn't make sense the first time around, and spend some time with it.

Day 65—Find other ARE candidates' prep notes.

Start using other peoples study notes that you can find on the Web. See the Resource Page at **YoungArchitect.com/AREbook**, FTP site, and forums.

Day 70—Jump back on the vignettes. Master them.

It's now time to hit the vignettes really hard. You should be uploading your practices, working on alternates, and commenting on other people's vignettes. Try to find tricks to help you solve it faster and ways to double-check your work. The goal is to have a 110 percent complete understanding on how to solve the vignette.

Day 73—Make big, bold studying moves with greater intensity.

Cancel your life for the next two weeks. Coincidently "get sick" because you have been studying too hard, and use some office sick time to push your studying farther ahead.

In all my testing experiences, how I used this time was critical in determining my success on the exam. Don't tell my boss.

Day 88—Stop studying.

To stop studying is much harder than you think. I always pulled the plug two days before the exam. I would try to relax and not think about it too much. I often failed at this, but the most I would do is review flashcards.

Day 90—Testing day.

Congratulations! You made it. You worked your ass off. You put in the time. There's always more that you could do. Relax. Be easy. Check out my blog post with advice for testing day—you can find the link on my resources page at **YoungArchitect.com/AREbook**.

Sometimes after a test, I'd feel great and would go back to the office. Other times, I'd feel like I just ran a mental marathon and need to sleep for three hours. Either way, I usually took the day off in case I needed it.

Day 91—Wash, rinse, and repeat until they are all done.

Repeat this schedule until all tests are done.

I wouldn't recommend taking too much time off between exams. Building momentum is incredibly hard. The most productive thing you could do is transition from taking one test into studying for the next test by starting this schedule again at Day 1.

What does your study schedule look like?

This is approximately the schedule that I used for most of my exams. Everyone has their own methodologies. Remember to do what works for you. If you want to hold yourself accountable to this kind of system, you could start a new calendar for your first exam right now. If you're feeling lost about the specific schedule you want to use, you could just go with the one I've laid out here. Either way, while you're studying, if something isn't working for you, change it. Then after you finish your first exam, re-evaluate and start the process over.

Finding a Study Space

I have watched a lot of people start studying for the Architect Registration Exam and never finish the process. One commonality that I think many of them have is that they do not have a solid place to get their studying done.

Where did I study?

There is a Starbucks six blocks away from my house, located next door to a local health food grocery store. The Starbucks has a big wood table perfect for spreading out all the papers, or even reading drawings. It has Wi-Fi, electrical outlets, and tons of college students who are also there to study. I purchased some nice headphones to help drown out all the terrible music Starbucks plays.

This worked for me. In fact, it is one of my secrets to success. Part of the reason I became an Architect is because I am hyper-sensitive to my environment. Once I started going to this specific Starbucks, the amount of work I was able to get done drastically increased.

In fact, since I finished the test, I never stopped showing up to Starbucks regularly. Instead of studying for the exam, I am now working on other things.

The problems with studying at home or the office

My home and office are not environments that were designed for studying. They are designed for living and working. Studying for an Architect Registration Exam is neither of those.

There are a million **distractions** at home and in the office, and the only person whom I can really blame for being distracted by these things is myself. The phone rings, an email comes in, the dog barks at something, or a contractor calls and needs an answer immediately because every minute is costing the client money. The task of studying often gets knocked down to the lowest priority. Suddenly, cleaning the refrigerator sounds a lot better than reading that chapter about structural diaphragms.

It's really easy to **lose track of time** at home. "Oh crap, its 4 p.m., and I have only completed one of the four things I needed to get done." I say that a lot. I don't know about you, but when I am at home, I feel like time moves exponentially faster than it does everywhere else. My weekends fly by. I"m used to it now. But even if I could study at home, since the clock moves faster there, I prefer to just not study there.

It's too personal. I liked to keep my studying out of the house and separate from the rest of my life. I never really mixed business or pleasure with my studying. Studying in the office or at home would have blurred that line. I also used a completely separate book bag for the ARE. After a while, I started thinking about the exam as if it were just another project.

Finding a place to study

It's not that hard. These are my requirements:

1. Access to food
2. A place to spread out all the papers
3. A bathroom
4. Access to caffeine
5. No drama

I live in Portland, Oregon, and not all coffee shops are the same. The places where the cool kids get their expensive coffee are kind of like bars that serve caffeine instead of booze. These coffee shops are the worst places for me to get anything done. The coffee shop scene here is soooo big that Starbucks is considered kinda lame; there isn't a lot of socializing, and it's perfect for working.

The advantage of studying somewhere other than home or the office

Sometimes the hardest part for me was walking out the front door to make the walk up to Starbucks. I always felt that after I arrived there, got comfortable, and ordered some caffeine, my brain quickly warmed up and knew what it was supposed to do. My brain subconsciously started getting really productive, just by being there.

It's easier to say, "I'm going to spend two hours at Starbucks and do as much as I can," than, "I'm going to read these next two chapters at home." You'll never get those two chapters read. At least I couldn't. I always measured my studying by time. How many actual hours was I at Starbucks studying during the week? Also, the time it took to walk to Starbucks didn't count.

Being removed from the home or the office makes studying become official. There is nothing going on in Starbucks where I could get distracted for 30 minutes.

The "spirit" of the place

When I was in architecture school and got stuck with a design, I used to go back to the physical locations where I sat in my previous design studios when I was doing really good work. As I sat in the same place, I would think about what was going on back then, as opposed to right now. Then I'd try to work out why my design was stuck.

Sometimes it was just a change of scenery. Doing this always helped me move through my problem.

I'm sure Steven Pressfield will agree with my theory.

By finding a comfortable place that is free of distractions, you will greatly improve your efficiency and ability to work through your ARE study material. Time is your most valuable resource when studying for the ARE—and you don't have any to waste.

Study Materials

When I first started studying for the Architecture Registration Exam, I had absolutely no idea where to begin. I spent the first few months running in circles, trying to just figure everything out and locate study materials for each exam. I remember looking at the A201-General Conditions document for the first time and being terrified and exhausted by the thought of having to memorize and understand this document.

Studying for the ARE requires reading an enormous amount of content regarding the profession. I very quickly learned there are no shortcuts. Luckily, I had a lot of practical knowledge from work experience. But I still really needed to study everything, some content areas more than others.

I learned that you can drastically accelerate the process by using the right tool for the job. Passing the exams requires branching out and using study materials from all over the place to get up to speed quicker on various topics.

The goal of this chapter is to give you an overview of the materials to help prevent you from going on the wild goose chase that I experienced, trying to prepare for each test. When you are first getting started, it takes some time to wrap your mind around the *process* of preparing for the exams, not just the actual studying.

The Big Two

The two biggest sources of study material for the Architect exam are put out by two different publishers, **Kaplan** and the **ARE Review Manual by David Kent Ballast**. Reading both Kaplan and Ballast was always the first place I started studying for each exam, and I used them both pretty extensively.

Internet forums often debate one over the other. In my experience, I learned that you really need both to get a holistic view of information required for each test. I read both books for all six divisions of the multiple choice exams. Often, one book proved to be more helpful than the other, depending on the subject matter. For each test topic, one book usually seemed too general, while the other was too detailed. So it was helpful to cross-reference between them. This made the most sense for me.

Links to all these materials can be found on my Resources page at **YoungArchitect.com/AREbook**.

Viewing Ballast as an Investment

I bought the Ballast book when I was halfway finished studying for my first test, CDS. I then literally used this book for every single remaining test of the Architect Registration Exam. I always tend to recommend that ARE candidates get their hands on this book sooner rather than later. It's kind of expensive, but definitely an investment in the process. If you're serious about becoming a Licensed Architect, it is just one small drop in the bucket.

I looked on the Internet, and there really isn't any decent review of this book, aside from the small blurbs in Amazon reviews. Since I tend to overthink everything, I wrote one. You can visit my Resources page at **YoungArchitect.com/ARebook** for my official review of the David Kent Ballast FAIA – Architect Registration Exam Review Manual.

I have literally used this book three dozen times over the past few years since my exams to look things up while at work. Often, I come across a problem that involves something I remember learning for the exam. Since architecture is a reference profession, I have the answer from Ballast in 30 seconds. The index for this book is awesome because it includes the entire exam; finding something that may overlap across multiple divisions (CDS, PPP and SPD) is super simple. Good luck doing the same with Kaplan, which treated each exam as its own book and used separate authors for each division.

Ballast also offers supplemental practice tests and vignette practice examples for each division. This information is really good, but the one thing to consider is that all the answers for these practice tests are literally written from the Ballast book. If you memorize the Ballast book like a robot, you'll do great on their practice test but probably just OK on the Kaplan tests. **YOU HAVE TO CROSS-REFERENCE THIS STUDY MATERIAL.** The Ballast book is great, but if you want to pass these tests, you need to use other books.

Kaplan

I often found Kaplan to be easier to read than Ballast. What I liked about using Kaplan was the end of each chapter concluded with a short quiz, testing me on the information I just learned.

Like most textbook publishers, Kaplan likes to publish new versions of their study guides almost every year. It's essentially the same book. Remember in college, they were constantly updating and rearranging the chapters of the textbooks so you had to buy the latest, most expensive copy?

This is a good thing because Amazon has used copies of those old study guides at a significant discount. Regardless of what Kaplan wants you to think, an ARE study guide from three years ago is just as relevant today. My advice is to buy the cheapest book, not the most current book.

If you purchase the Kaplan books, I wouldn't recommend purchasing their vignette info or flashcards that are sold separately. I always reviewed it but never really found the vignette info that useful. The Kaplan flashcards appeared to be flashcards directly from the glossary. I made my own flashcards of that information as part of my flashcards for each test.

For more detailed information on Kaplan, visit the links on my Resources page at **YoungArchitect.com/ARebook.** I provide links to all the editions to the Kaplan Guides on Amazon to help you find the best price.

Architect Exam Prep

Architect Exam Prep (AEP) is new on the ARE scene. They started putting out products for exams that I had completed just as I was wrapping up my last few exams. At the moment, they have products for six of seven sections. Each exam package is $100, and I must say it looks like they give you a TON of material to help you pass each section.

After you purchase, everything is downloaded, and there are no actual, physical products or CDs. I purchased the whole CDS enchilada and wrote a very thorough review of what is inside this package. Check out my Resources page at **YoungArchitect.com/ARebook** for the link to the AEP Review.

The study guide is central to Architect Exam Prep. It is the meat and potatoes of the AEP. It includes the flashcards and practice tests. The study guide is outlined in the same format as the NCARB study guide, using the same criteria that NCARB uses to grade the test. If you fail the AEP practice exam, you will know what area you need to spend more time studying. AEP is the only major study material guide to provide the content in this format.

AEP also offers audio MP3 files to listen to. The audio is awesome! I listened to chapters after I read them in the study guide and found the audio significantly easier to follow after I had read the corresponding chapter. This kind of audio would have been really helpful when I was studying for my exams. It allows you to take in information when you're out and about. I could have listened when I was running or walking the dog,

How To Pass The Architecture Registration Exam

thus accelerating my studying time.

Ballast Practice Exams

Ballast publishes practice exams separately from their ARE Review Manual. All the content for the practice exams is taken directly from the ARE Review Manual. Each practice exam book also includes vignette sample problems that you can work out on paper.

The Ballast practice exam books are really good, and I highly recommend using them. Check out my blogpost about how I used practice exams more as a study tool, rather than a practice exam.

Gang Chen's Mock ARE Exam

I used Gang Chen's books on my last few exams and found them to be extremely helpful. His books consist of a practice exam and a step-by-step guide through the graphic vignettes. He brought a lot of value for the Building Systems test that really helped me understand how to do the calculations, rather than be intimidated by them. I wish he had published his materials several years earlier. I recently wrote a review of what Gang Chen offers in his mock ARE exam. Check out the Resources page for a link.

MEEB

MEEB is the best. I really got a lot from MEEB. It is a very intimidating book because it's two-and-a-half inches thick. MEEB is super-detailed and thorough. I used an old copy of MEEB that I borrowed from a friend. Someone put together this chart outlining where all of the MEEB chapters can be found and what you should study. I pretty much followed this chart verbatim. There are also free practice quizzes online. MEEB is also the only textbook that I know of that has its own music video. I provide links to the practice quizzes on my the Resources page.

The NCARB Study Guides

I studied a lot of old material from the ARE 3.1 that was useful. Just be careful, as codes, agencies, building technology, sustainability, ADA, and AIA docs have evolved since that information was published. If you find material from Architectural Licensing Seminars (ALS), this is basically the old version of Kaplan. Kaplan bought ALS many years ago and rebranded it with their name on it. The NCARB 3.1 ARE study guides are also still very relevant.

NCARB has their own study guide, which predominately focuses on the breakdown (percentages) of 'Content Areas' for each exam. It provided a helpful overview of content, and it helped me understand passing vs. failing solutions to work through vignettes. The practice test included the answers but did not include explanations for the answers, which wasn't much help as a "study guide." NCARB gives a list of books as recommended reading. I actually disagree with all of their lists and think that if you only read the books they recommend, you will not pass the ARE.

Frank Ching - Building Codes Illustrated

Ching's Building Codes Illustrated was extremely helpful in demystifying the International Building Code. It taught me how to get through the language barrier that I often struggle with regarding how the IBC is written. I highly recommend buying this book and reading it immediately.

I bought A Global History of Architecture to study architectural history. I love architectural history, and I am a huge fan of Frank Ching. So the ARE gave me an excuse to buy this awesome book.

Frank Ching has been one of my greatest architecture teachers since the very moment I decided to become an architect many years ago. I own every single book of his and recently listed them all on the Architecture Student's Christmas list. Ching's books are incredible reference guides and should be on every architect's bookshelf.

YouTube

I used YouTube quite a bit to find videos about whatever topic I happened to be studying. I would typically search for whatever topic I was studying at the time. Sometimes it's easier to watch TV (YouTube) than it is to read a book.

Professor Norman Dorf

Professor Dorf passed away in 2007, shortly after he published his book and recorded the video series. I bought his book called Solutions and used it for every single exam. It's a great book, and I would almost always use his method as a starting point. His book also has practice vignettes that are really good.

In his video series, he breaks it down step-by-step with his methodology to passing each vignette. I purchased his videos for my first test CDS, and it was really good. It got me up and running very quickly. As I moved through the exams, I felt I didn't need the video, but I would highly recommend them to anyone who is struggling with understanding a vignette.

ARE Advisor

I really like the ARE Advisor product. He takes the ARE Practice vignettes and, in a very organized manner, breaks them down into easy to understand, step-by-step directions showing how to arrive at the solution.

The NCARB Study Guides really do not tell you much. They just show you the passing and failing solution and say absolutely nothing about arriving there. The ARE Advisor has taken the mystery out of getting from Point A to Point B. I wish this product had been around several years ago to hold my hand through learning the practice vignettes. I always struggled when I started to learn each vignette and essentially figured it out through a ton of trial and error.

He charges $100 for all 7 divisions, which in my opinion is pretty cheap, compared to Dorf.

Ballast and Kaplan Practice Vignettes

I used both Ballast and Kaplan heavily during the exams for the multiple choice sections. I always felt like the other resources were much better at discussing the vignettes. Ballast writes about vignettes in the ARE Review manual, and it"s OK. Then he gives practice alternates separately in the practice exam books. Kaplan sells their vignette info separately from the multiple choice material.

I highly recommend the Ballast Practice Exam Books over the Kaplan vignette information. I always looked at the Kaplan stuff because I already had it, but the material isn't that great on the topic of vignettes.

Ultimate List of ARE Study Materials

I've written a more detailed comprehensive, three-part post about all of this on YoungArchitect.com. In **Part 1**, I discuss products that I used for all 7 exams. In I list and review every single study material I used for all exams.. Lastly **Part 3** is all about the the graphic exams. Check out my Resources page for the links to those blog posts.

The most important thing to know about ARE-specific study materials

Architect Exam Prep, Ballast, and Kaplan are only starting points. **None** of them is a magic bullet on their own.

You really must supplement with other resources to get a better understanding and strengthen your odds of passing the exam. You are the only one who is going to know what areas you need the most help with, and you can't know this until after you have spent some time with the ARE-specific study materials.

I strongly recommend spending time with the ARE-Specific Study Materials prior to supplementing.

Again, to save you a whole bunch of time, I've posted links to all materials and blog posts that have been referenced in this chapter on my Resources page at **YoungArchitect.com/AREblog.**

Practice Exams

I didn't understand the value of practice exams until I was halfway done with the Architecture Registration Exam. Had I understood their value from the beginning, I could have saved a significant amount of frustration.

Eventually, I got my hands on every single ARE practice test I could. I spent a lot of money on ARE practice exam books. I think they are absolutely fundamental for studying and learning how to pass these difficult tests.

Practice exams kept me from going insane by breaking up the immense amount of required reading. I used to go to Starbucks at lunch and work on practice exams for an hour or so and then go back to office. This allowed me to get some very effective studying done in a short period of time, because the practice questions engaged me and forced me to utilize memory recall. This was huge for me.

Practice exams kept my studying engaged, awake, and moving.

How I used ARE practice tests

Most people like to sit down and create a mock ARE testing scenario, working through 100-150 questions and looking up all the answers at the end. This is great. I did this too, but only at the end of my studying.

I used the practice tests more as a studying tool. They helped me create a much more powerful, efficient method of studying. When using the practice exams, I would only work on three questions at a time, and then I'd go look up the answers.

By keeping the practice exams to a three-question max, it kept the process of recalling information fresh in my brain. I could then have a better understanding of why I chose the answer that I did.

> If I **gave the wrong answer**, I would spend a few minutes understanding why I chose the wrong answer and why my thought process led me to choosing the wrong answer.

If I **confidently gave the right answer**, I would move onto the next question.

If I **unconfidently gave the right answer**, I would process the question and answer and try to bring more confidence to my thought process.

No practice exam is ever a substitute for the test

Practice exam questions are always derived from the study material that they originated from.

Say you spend a lot of time **only studying the Ballast book** and no other ARE material. If you take a Ballast practice exam, you'll do great.

Say you study all the other ARE study materials and **do not use** the Ballast book. If you take a Ballast practice exam, you may not do so well.

I'm picking on Ballast, but this applies to all ARE study materials. Whoever is writing the study materials you are reading has their own opinions on what they think practice questions should be. They will always derive their questions from the content that they wrote.

This is why I always recommend that you use multiple sources of ARE study material.

Without disclosing any content from the exam, I'll guarantee that you will see questions that have nothing to do with the test you are taking or studied for.

You will also encounter very strangely worded and confusing questions.

No authors of ARE study material could ever really re-create the real exam, but they definitely do a great job of trying and getting you in shape to take the exam.

Getting into the rhythm of answering questions

Reading ARE study books for hours and hours is only mental **information input**.

The test is about **recalling information** at a moment's notice.

Answering questions to recall information takes a lot of practice. It forces your brain to work in an opposite direction.

NCARB is constantly trying to trick you into choosing the wrong answer on an easy question. It takes practice to learn how to slow down and say, "What are they really asking about?," rather than just choosing an answer.

I had a really hard time slowing down, reading each question carefully, thinking about what is being asked, and choosing the right answer. I would frequently choose the wrong answer because I didn't read the question carefully enough.

Is English your second language? Practice exams could really help you.

I have a friend who moved to America in his early 20s for architecture school, and English isn't his native language. He is an extremely intelligent guy with an incredible work ethic. He put in his time studying and had all the knowledge to pass the test, but he kept doing poorly because he was getting tripped up on the linguistics of the questions.

English is my first (and only) language, and I very frequently was confused with trying to understand what NCARB was really asking because of the way questions were worded. If English is your second language, you may want to consider this and spend extra time answering practice questions.

The old stuff works

For ARE versions 3.1 and older, there was a company named Architectural Licensing Seminars (ALS). They were purchased by Kaplan, and then their content morphed into the Kaplan guides we have today.

I found a few of their old practice exams on a dusty old shelf in my local AIA office a long time ago. Even though it's old content, I thought it was really useful and helpful.

Start practice exams after the first pass

I wouldn't start using the practice exams until I made my first complete pass through one study guide. For me, this meant reading all the chapters of Ballast or Kaplan before I started working on practice questions. I was not going to spend time working on questions that I hadn''t yet encountered in the material.

Easy to carry around

Here's a practice question for you:

> **Question:** What do a brick and the Ballast book have in common?
>
> **Answer:** They both weigh about 5 pounds.

Practice exams are significantly less paper and much easier to carry around while walking and commuting. I brought them with me to work every day.

Practice, Practice, Practice

In the spirit of practice exams, here's a summary of the ways they could benefit you, as well as a few reminders to help you use them effectively.

Practice exams can be especially helpful:

- For getting into the rhythm of answering questions;
- For providing a break from reading;
- For working on memory recall;
- For improving study efficiency;
- If English is your second language; and
- If you want study aids that are easy to carry around.

Things to remember about practice exams:

- No practice exam is ever a substitute for the test;
- The old stuff works; and
- Start practice exams after your first pass through the study material.

Flashcards

Are you using them already? If not, I want to encourage you to try using them.

While I was taking the ARE, making, using and obsessing over my flashcards became fundamental to uploading the massive amount of necessary information into my head. After finishing my second test, I realized that flashcards were a very powerful tool, and I relied on them a lot.

Everybody has their own strengths and weaknesses. Some tools work a lot better for some than for others. As we have discussed in previous chapters, the real power is finding the learning systems, processes, and techniques that are the most effective for you. Use what works to get these exams behind you.

Notebooks vs. Flashcards

When I started studying, I used to read Ballast and kept a notebook with all the important notes that I needed to memorize. As I refined my study method, I started to realize that the notebook was the worst place to keep this information. This was the problem I was having:

- The 8.5 x 11 format of the notebook felt too formal for the onslaught of data I was trying to digest. It also wasn't very accessible.
- I would frequently fill pages with a lot of unrelated information. One page would have several big ideas on it, and when I looked at it again, it would confuse me. The chronology of how the information was captured on the page also didn't help.
- Your friend JennyPDX already created a beautiful set of notes for the ARE. She already did the leg work of extracting all the key information. Why spend time recreating her masterpiece?

    (Disclaimer: Jenny's notes are awesome, but they cliff notes. They aren't a substitute for actually reading the books and learning the material)

The flashcards win

Very quickly, I abandoned using notebooks and started keeping everything on flashcards without ever looking back.

I used to buy big stacks of blank 3 x 5 flashcards and used the office hole-puncher to put a hole in the top left corner. Then I'd keep them bound by a giant metal ring.

Anytime I saw something I didn't already know but needed to learn, it became a flashcard. That was how I decided what gets put on a card. All of the terms, concepts, ideas, definitions, formulas—I put each one on a flashcard and added it to the pile.

Flashcards allowed me to extract the important stuff from everything else on the page and to think about it independently—as opposed to Ballast, which is soo concentrated that it has too many big (and hard to digest) ideas on a single page.

To kick off each new test, I would first go to Ballast and Kaplan and extract all of the definitions, formulas, and key information into flashcards. Then I'd start actually reading the material. Definitions were always a good place for me to start. If I could get those nailed down sooner rather than later, it made studying a lot easier. I also didn't need to carry around that five-pound Ballast book, which really only contained one-seventh of the information applicable to what I was actually working on.

Flashcards everywhere! Hundreds of them!

I kept flashcards everywhere. I used to review them while I waited for and rode the bus to work. They were in my office and in my various coat pockets and book bags. And maybe sometimes (dare I say it?), I would look at them in the bathroom. I stuffed my books with blank flashcards, just in case I saw something that needed to be memorized later.

About once a week or so, I would go through huge stacks of flashcards and find all of the cards I hadn't fully digested. Then I could work on them a bit more.

The Kaplan and Archiflash flashcards

When I started studying for my first exam (CDS), I checked out the Kaplan Flashcards that my AIA had available to ARE candidates. Those cards were for ARE 3.1. I found that the Kaplan flashcards are nothing more than the glossary for each division, just on a glossy card.

This is what inspired me to start making my own flashcards. I thought to myself, "Great,

I could just make these myself in a language that I can understand." I have never actually used the Archiflash cards. I became so obsessed with making my own cards that I was in my own world. I never paid Archiflash cards any attention. Many people have spoken very highly of them, so I'm sure they are worth checking out.

Just do what works

Passing these exams is an enormous endeavor. Whether flashcards are for you or not is basically irrelevant. Anyone who is struggling with these exams needs to **examine what is and isn't working with how they are studying.**

Beating the Vignettes

Contrary to what NCARB or anyone else says, the core essence of the vignettes is testing your ability to do three things:

1. **Follow directions;**
2. **Recognize and respond to key information; and**
3. **Hack out a graphic solution with the NCARB software.**

Anyone can learn how to do these vignettes with enough practice. It's really just an architectural video game. I don't believe having a fancy architecture degree or being an all-star in design studio are prerequisites to succeeding at the vignettes. In fact, I believe those qualifications may actually make it harder for you.

Throw out what you already know

One of the best things you can do when you are working on vignettes is to **forget everything you already know about CAD, codes, design, and construction.** NCARB has a very specific way of how they want things done. Many times, **the way NCARB wants to see it done conflicts with real world knowledge**. This is where it goes back to following directions.

The Essential Process

Looking back, this was my process for learning the vignettes:

1. **Always start sooner than later.** Don't wait until the last minute. Some vignettes are harder than others. Don't assume you won't need a lot of time on a vignette because of your previous vignette history.

2. **Start drawing the vignettes by looking at the solution and copying it.** This

allowed me to get comfortable drawing it and learn to use the tools without frustration.

3. **Practice solving the solution differently than NCARB's correct answer.** Focus on understanding all the different elements.

4. **Start posting your solutions online and commenting on others'.** Participation in the online discussion is key to passing the vignettes.

5. **Practice other versions and post them.** Get your hands on the 3.1 version, alternates, Dorf, Ballast, Kaplan, or any other alternate vignette you can find.

6. **Look for opportunities to simplify, speed up, and cross- or double-check your work.** Look up other people's step-by-step solutions to see what you can learn from their methodologies.

Tips for the vignettes

Use Practice Vignettes

A lot of ARE study guides have alternate vignettes printed inside for you to tape up to your drafting table and work out with your drafting pencils, triangles and T-square. I would typically just solve these on a sheet of tracing paper in a coffee shop. My method was to copy the basic shapes onto little pieces of tracing paper, lay out the pieces and then trace a new clean copy.

My goal in doing this was to practice understanding the program and finding solutions. I wouldn't worry so much about the accuracy or the details.

Make a feet-to-inches conversion chart

```
3'-0" = 36"      11'-0" = 132"     CONVERSION CHART
3'-6" = 42"      11'-6" = 138"     HTTP://YoungARCHITECT.ORG/ARE
4'-0" = 48"      12'-0" = 144"
4'-6" = 54"      12'-6" = 150"
5'-0" = 60"      13'-0" = 156"
5'-6" = 66"      13'-6" = 162"
6'-0" = 72"      14'-0" = 168"

6'-6" = 78"      14'-6" = 174"
7'-0" = 84"      15'-0" = 180"
7'-6" = 90"      15'-6" = 186"
8'-0" = 96"      16'-0" = 192"

8'-6" = 102      16'-6" = 198"
9'-0" = 108"     17'-0" = 204"
9'-6 = 114"
10'-0 = 120"
10'-6" = 126"
```

One area of the vignette that would always slow me down is converting back and forth to inches.

For example:

What is 103" in feet and inches?

How many inches is 14'-9"?

How long did it take you to get those answers?

These calculations drove me nuts, because there are lots of them and they interrupted my thought process. They also left tons of room for sloppy math errors. Before the clock started, I made a conversion chart in 6" increments. This allowed me to quickly look up what 103" is, rather than do the math. It also allowed me to choose between doing the calculations in either feet and inches or inches only, using whatever was easier to solve the problem.

I was always so stressed out during my exams and eliminating these small calculations by making a conversion chart it took another worry off my list. I would typically make these charts before I took the multiple choice portion—they are also useful for answering the multiple choice questions.

Make a vignette chart and fill in the blanks

Charts were huge for me on site planning and the SD vignettes. I would draw a chart and, as I read the program, I would just fill in the blanks. Using a chart to understand how all the pieces came together made the design step go soo much faster. The chart was also key when it came to double-checking my work.

How To Pass The Architecture Registration Exam

BUILDING + HEIGHTS	VIEW OF	CLOSE TO / FAR APART	ORIENTATION	SUN, WIND SHADING	OTHER CRITERIA
OFFICE TOWER 60' ①		POND ① LESS THAN 125'	ENTRANCE VISIBLE TO BENTLEY ① ENTRANCE ON PLAZA ③		
RESTAURANT 20' ②	POND ⑤	OFFICE TOWER AT LEAST 210' APART ⑪			④ BLOCK VIEW OF SERVICE ENTRANCE FROM THE PLAZA ⑩ PROVIDE CIRCULATION TO SERVICE ENTRANCE
PEDESTRIAN PLAZA 8000 SF ③				NOON SUMMER SUN/NO SHADE ⑥ BLOCK PREVAILING WIND ⑦	⑤ MAIN ENT OF OFFICE TOWER ON PLAZA ⑫ CONNECT TO HC PARKING
PARKING ⑤ 33 SPOTS 30 STANDARD 9×18 3 HC 12×18		HC WITHIN 100' OF OFFICE ENTRANCE ⑧ CONNECT HC TO PP ⑫			
OTHER DRIVEWAY ⑨ PERPENDICULAR FIRST 20' CURBOUT IS MIN 120' FROM INTERSECTION ⑩ TREE = 50' ⑬					CODE ⑬ - NO CLOSER THAN 5' TO BLDG - 20' BLDG SEPERATION - 30' POND SETBACK - KILL 6 TREES ONLY

Here's how I organized it:

> **Horizontally** across the top, I included the program and code requirements: View of, Close to, Orientation, Sun/Wind or Shading Requirements and any other comments or notes.

> **Vertically** across the left side of the page, I included all the different building elements and heights. I'd then fill in the requirements for each building as they are presented in the program.

To save time, I would also draw the ADA door clearance diagram. When I got to that part in the program I could just fill in the dimensions on my sketch.

Charts were huge for me during the SD vignette. I developed my own fool-proof method that made it really hard to mess up. Unfortunately it wasn't fool-proof enough, because after I passed the exam I tossed all my SD notes. Now I can hardly remember how to make that chart.

Use the numbers from the program in your notes

The program is numbered. When I would copy it onto my scratch paper, I would also write the number of where I got that information in the program. This allowed me to know exactly where to go if I had a question about something I wrote on my scratch paper. You can see how I did this in the site planning chart that I referenced above.

Alternates are your best friend

Alternate vignettes helped me tremendously. It took me a little while to get the hang of how the alternates worked, so let me try to explain it.

When you install the NCARB software onto your computer, it installs a folder (C:\Program Files\NCARB) onto your hard drive. That folder includes all files associated with running the software. There is a DWG file that is essentially the base drawing for each vignette. If you go into the folder and swap out the DWG file with one of the alternates, you can now practice an alternate vignette.

Also, don't forget to also use the old ARE 3.1 version for more vignette practice. That software can also be found on the FTP site.

How to post your vignettes online

After you finish the vignette you'll need a graphic that you can post online. The best way to do this is by hitting Alt+Print Screen button on your keyboard to take a picture of your screen. Then go over to MS Paint, which is usually located from going to: Windows Start Button>All Programs>Accessories>Paint. Once inside paint you can paste (Cntrl-V) the solution, save it to JPG and upload it to a forum.

The MS Paint method always seemed to work the best. I've tried using Photoshop and couldn't seem to ever get the image size to display properly on the forum and never learned why.

You may need an old computer

Just getting the software to run on a computer is the first battle. The NCARB practice software doesn't really run on any other operating system other than Windows XP. It works OK on Windows 7, although it will not allow you to toggle back and forth to the program.

Here's a list of all the things I did to work around this issue.

1. **Get an old computer that runs Windows XP just for practicing the vignettes.** It will allow you to have easy access to all the alternates. I used an old laptop until it died. Then I bought a cheap hand-me-down laptop with Windows XP so I could finish the exam.
2. **Install Windows XP on your Apple computer as a remote desktop.** Several years ago, I used software called Parallels when I did this. This method worked for a little while, but was kind of a pain the butt. Eventually that computer died, so I was back to square one.
3. **Download Windows XP mode for Windows 7.** Since my desktop had Windows 7, Microsoft gave me software to run Windows XP as a remote desktop. It essentially runs XP as a piece of software and allows you to run other software inside of that. This worked great and handled the NCARB software stunningly. I've provided a link to this information on my Resources page at **YoungArchitect.com/AREbook.** If you get stuck, I can't help you. You're on your own. I"m not an IT guy.
4. **Pay NCARB to use the practice software Web site.** You can log into NCARB's Web site and access a remote desktop that has the software loaded onto it. I tried this when it first came out and was very disappointed with the quality, even though I tried it on many different computers. The software felt slow and klunky and I couldn't load in alternates, so I gave up on it. This may work just fine for your situation, so I would encourage you to explore this option.

Commenting on other people's vignettes will accelerate your learning curve

Right now, there are a handful of people trying to learn the same vignette you are—and they are all talking about it on the Internet. You're shooting yourself in the foot if you're not using this online community to help you with your vignettes.

Reviewing other peoples vignettes, pointing out errors, asking questions and talking about the vignette is the very best thing you could possibly be doing, **next to practicing.** I always started commenting and participating in the conversation about the vignettes when I was about 40 percent of the way to complete understanding. Any question that you may have has most likely already been asked, and everyone online is very helpful. You also need to help get the people who are behind up to speed.

I firmly believe in **the principle of helping and teaching others as a tool for deeper learning and understanding**. The online forums are excellent examples of how this works. If you are reading or using the forums to get information, you need to give back when you have information that could help others.

Using sketch rectangles and sketch circles to measure things

Professor Dorf likes to use sketch circles A LOT to lay things out—such as finding the floor-to-floor dimension in the building section vignette. I found that using sketch rectangles is much more accurate and leaves less room for error. The software is clunky and determining the top of a circle can be much more tedious than determining the top of a rectangle. Every situation is different, and one shape usually lends itself better to accomplishing the same thing.

Triple-check your work

I can't stress this enough. Especially for the calculations. As you develop your method, find moments to check your work before you move to the next step. For example, **triple-check all your calculations before you start drawing the stair.**

At the end of each exam, I would also click on the draw button and go through each element to make sure it was used and nothing is being forgotten. It could be something easy, like forgetting to draw a grade line in the building section vignette. Forgetting the grade line will cause you to fail the entire exam. It seems silly, but without the grade line, you don't know how deep the footings are. If the footings aren't deep enough, it is a fatal error.

Don't use other people's standards

Everyone learns differently. When someone says, **"This vignette was easy. I only spent five hours learning it and I aced the test."** That doesn't mean it will take you five hours. It realistically could take you twice that amount of time. You just don't know.

All the vignettes are different—and some are a lot harder than others. Always start working on the vignettes as soon as you start studying for that test. If you wait until the last minute, you will fail the test. They aren't hard, but they do take a lot of practice.

Hacking the MC Questions

Multiple choice questions make up a huge percentage of the ARE. Given this, you really need to ramp up your answering skills when it comes to these types of questions. There are a couple of things to take notice of when it comes to multiple choice questions.

First, consider what kind of test-taker you have been in the past. Do you rush through exams, or are you the last one to turn yours in? This is knowledge that you need to have in order to effectively beat the multiple choice questions.

If you're the student that rushes through the exam, you need to slow down. If you're the student that is obsessive and indecisive about every question, you need lay off the OCD tendencies and be more strategic in choosing your answers.

Multiple choice questions can be tricky, and they are designed to confuse you. You must take your time reading the question AND all of the possible answers.

In addition to taking your time understanding the question and answer possibilities, there are other strategies to help you choose the best answer.

Think about how NCARB would want you to answer this question.

Practice tests will help you learn how NCARB asks questions, and you will gain a better understanding of how best to answer them

Eliminate the answer that is absolutely incorrect.

If something is obviously a bogus answer just eliminate the possibility right away.

Dissect the question for specific information to help you determine the answer.
- Is there a specific location within the question that would impact the answer?
- Does time play a part in the question?
- Does the phase of the project play a part in the question?
    - Is there a sequence of events within the question?

How To Pass The Architecture Registration Exam

- Are cause and effect a part of the question?
* Is one answer going to be similar to another answer?
* Can you work the question backward? (This is mostly applicable in questions that involve math.)
* If none of the above applies, do your best to choose the answer that you think NCARB would want you to choose.

Here is a breakdown of how to work through this thought process on a simple question:

A dog:

A. Is a Labrador Retriever.

B. Is a mammal.

C. Eats Alpo.

D. Is furry and wags its tail.

When first reading this question, it may appear that all of the answers could be correct. To break this down, you would re-read the question and each possible answer.

A dog (A) is a Labrador Retriever. True, Golden Retrievers are a breed of dog. However, not all dogs are Golden Retrievers. This may not be the best answer.

A dog (B) is a mammal. Dogs are definitely mammals. Nothing else to add here.

A dog (C) eats Alpo. True, dogs eat Alpo, but not all dogs eat Alpo. Not sure if this is the correct answer, given that some dogs may not like Alpo.

A dog (D) is furry and wags its tail. Well, most dogs are furry, but there are hairless dogs. And not all dogs have tails. Not sure this answer is correct because this statement cannot apply to all dogs.

So now that we have broken down every possible answer, we can say with certainty that the best answer is (B) A dog is a mammal.

Now, this is a very straightforward and simple question. You will certainly see more challenging questions on the ARE. However, this introduces you to the process of breaking down the question to find the best answer.

Now, let's take a more challenging question.

Which of the following would be the best design-with-climate strategy in the layout of a new town in a cool region such as Winnipeg or Minneapolis?

    A. *The town structure should be densely grouped; larger building units may be grouped close together but spaced to utilize sun-heat effects, and the layout should provide a sheltering effect against winds.*

    B. *The preferred design is an open and free layout of buildings that tend to merge with nature.*

    C. *The town structure should be dense and provide shade, and unit dwellings or groups of buildings should create court-like areas.*

    D. *Buildings should be separated to utilize air movements, and the character of the town fabric should be loose and scattered*

Let's break down the question.

What is it asking for: The best design with climate strategy?

Clues to finding the right answer:

Best design-with-climate strategy—This means the design works with the climate of the region. A building designed to be in Arizona would not work if you took the same building and put it in the mountains of Colorado.

Cool region such as Winnipeg or Minneapolis—A cool region means it's cold and windy. The other regions in the U.S, are Temperate, Hot Arid and Hot Humid. What do I remember about cold regions? I remember that one of the goals is to minimize exterior walls to take advantage of interior heat and minimize the heat loss in exterior walls. I remember learning about how temperature and wind-chill are completely separate. Wind on a building in a cold climate can make it much colder than the temperature.

Let's break down each answer.

A. The town structure should be **densely grouped**; larger building units may be **grouped close together** but **spaced to utilize sun-heat effects**, and the layout should **provide a sheltering effect** against winds.

The words "densely grouped" reminds me that while designing in a cool climate, the goal should be to minimize building envelope to minimize the heat loss. Designs are often compact and insulated.

Grouped close together makes sense because it's cold.

Spaced to utilize the sun-heat effects makes sense, so they aren't casting a shadow on themselves.

Provide sheltering from wind. I remember learning about putting trees upwind from the structure to diffuse the wind before it arrives at the building.

This is a good answer. All parts seem to make sense.

B. The preferred design is an **open and free layout** of buildings that tend to **merge with nature.**

Open and free layout? This doesn't sound right for a cold region where there is cold snow and wind. It sounds like it could be for more of a hot climate.

Merge with nature—maybe to protect from the wind, but it's cold. So it's not like they need shade to make it colder. Low confidence in this answer.

C. The town structure should be **dense and provide shade**, and unit dwellings or groups of buildings should **create court-like areas**.

Dense and provide shade—a dense structure makes sense, but the shade doesn't.

It's already cold. It doesn't need to be colder.

Create court-like areas—What is a court? It's an open space that is enclosed on all four sides. A court will mean that at least one part of it will be shady at some point during the day. This doesn"t sound as good as "**spaced to utilize sun-heat effects** " from answer A. Not sure if this is an effective design strategy for a cold climate.

This answer is too much about shade. Creating shade is not something you want in a cold climate.

> D. Buildings should be **separated to utilize air movements**, and the **character of the town fabric should be loose and scattered.**

Separated to utilize air movements—the air is cold. Why would you want to move cold air around your building?

Character of the town fabric should be loose and scattered – This part could be true for a cold climate.

Only 50 percent of this answer good.

By process of elimination, answer A is the most appropriate answer.

The multiple choice questions of the ARE can be beat by:
- Taking the time to read the question and understand all the possible answers;
- Dissecting each possible answer for specific information;
- Choosing the most appropriate answer; and
- When all else fails, choosing the answer you feel NCARB would want you to choose.

Multiple choice questions are not designed to trick you—they're designed to make you think and to challenge you. You can beat them if you prepare, think logically, and don't get caught up in the nerves of the exam.

Part 5
Taking The Test

Test Day Tips

For months, you have been studying for the Architecture Registration Exam—reading books, practicing the vignettes and preparing for this day. ARE test day is extremely exhausting. Even though you are just sitting there in front of a computer for 4-5 hours, after it's all over, you will feel like you just ran a mental marathon. I always took the day off. Sometimes I even took a nap in the car before I left the parking lot.

During my many trips to the testing facility, I learned a few things that really helped me get through the day.

Be really nice to the people who work there and follow all their rules

This is my most important advice. You will see these people at least seven times. I learned their names and killed them with kindness at each visit.

Prometric (the company that administers the exam) has a laundry list of rules to make sure no one cheats on a test inside their facility. They will make you empty your pockets and show your ID each time you exit or enter the room.

The people who work there didn't write the rules and are just doing their jobs. Other exam takers are constantly giving them a hard time about the rules. They usually only visit the testing facility once in their life. As an ARE candidate, you will be seeing these people over and over.

Also, don't look at your phone on break. It's a rule that no one follows and it drives the Prometric staff crazy. It's not worth jeopardizing the test and all your studying.

Learn what page your name is on

Each time you enter or exit the room, they make you sign in and out of their notebook.

Take note of what page your name is on. Then you can say, "My name is on page 4," instead of waiting for them to flip through the notebook looking for it, while your testing clock is running.

Ask where you are sitting before you sit down

My exam center had eastern facing windows that were really distracting in the middle of the summer. There were also several testing booths that had A/C vents blasting out of them. All year long, that room was freezing. If you don't like where you are being placed before you take the exam, they can move you. However, after you start the exam clock, they can't really help you.

Better to be early than late

Prometric schedules from the morning up. If you are late, fitting you in can jeopardize someone who is scheduled after you. If you are early and they can fit you in, you get out of there earlier, making their day easier. Being 30 minutes, or even an hour, early was always OK at my testing center.

Bring food

Bring a lunch that you can scarf down in less than 15 minutes. My brain works better when I eat lightly. I would typically bring a salad and some fruit. A big, heavy lunch that takes forever to eat and digest and makes you want to take a nap wouldn't be good.

Take advantage of time during the boilerplate testing review

The first 10 minutes of the exam is dedicated to reviewing how the test works, as well as the NCARB Confidentiality Agreement. After I was done reviewing this information, I would use the remainder of this time to make charts on my scratch paper for the vignettes and the checkmark method. If you need a refresher on how I made my charts, please review the "Beating the Vignettes" chapter.

The checkmark method

If the test had 100 questions, I would fold up a piece of scrap paper and neatly write 1-100 on it. As I answered a question I was positive I got correct, I would place a "**+**" next to that question number. If I was clueless or basically guessed the answer, I would place a "-" symbol. If I was 50/50, I would place a checkmark. At the end of the exam after all the clocks have stopped, I would tally up these scores. I typically used 60/40 on the check marks, assuming that 60 percent were correct and 40 percent were incorrect.

Using this method gave me peace of mind and helped me to measure how I thought I did until I received my test score. I started using this method on all exams, but I abandoned this strategy several times if it became clear I was passing or failing the test. Looking back, it was always pretty accurate.

Make multiple laps around the exam

After taking the exam a few times, I learned that I kept getting freaked out by the first 20 questions. Eventually I learned to stop taking those first few questions so seriously. I started to use this methodology with the multiple choice questions.

The first pass is the least important. I would casually look at each question and only answer it if it was super easy. If it required too much thinking, I would just move onto the next question. I would confidently tell myself, "I know all the answers, but I will answer this later." This allowed me to get into the rhythm of quickly answering questions, which was huge for me.

Sometimes the wording of one question would help give the answer to another question. Moving through the exam several times allowed me to make these connections. I always just needed to warm up to answer the questions, and that damn clock always freaked me out. By the end of the exam, I would flip through enough questions to learn that everything that I was intimidated by in the beginning was really no big deal at all.

Mark all calculations or WTF questions

On the exam you can mark (more like tag) a question to be reviewed later. I would typically tag all WTF questions and lengthy calculations. Then I'd tackle these with the remaining time after I tackled all the other questions.

You cannot reschedule your test 0-3 business days before the exam

Saturday and Sundays are not considered business days, even if your testing center is open.

If your test is at noon on Tuesday, you will need to reschedule before noon on the previous Thursday.

I embarrassingly screwed this one up for BDCS. I decided to just show up with about half of the studying done and didn't do so hot.

The scores are available before you get the email

Not sure if this is good advice, but anyway, here goes. NCARB releases your score on its Web site many hours before you receive an email saying that your score is ready. I became obsessive, checking the Web site for my last test score and actually found out at 3 a.m. PST when I got up to go to the restroom.

I got my last test score eight days after the exam. Before they upgraded the process (Summer 2013), it used to take 3-4 weeks to get a test score.

Celebrate

After you are finished, congratulate yourself for taking the exam. It's a lot of hard work, and you're already winning by getting to this point and showing up.

Failing the Exam

Failing an exam actually isn't as big of a deal as you may think. Take it from me, I feel sheepish to (and probably shouldn't) admit this, but I failed the Architect exam **FOUR** different times. Yep, one, two, three, four times. And here I am, still hanging around. Eventually, I did pass them all and am now a Licensed Architect with my stamp in hand.

Why did you fail?

Failing your ARE could have happened for a number of really good reasons. Here's a list of reasons that I noticed going on with my own fails, as well as my friends' fails.

Just not having it together

Maybe you gave yourself five weeks to study when you really needed eight. This is the No. 1 reason why most people fail. Looking back, it's the best reason to fail the exam because it can be easily remedied the next time around.

You were dead-on-arrival

Site Planning and Design was my third test. When I took it, I had a lot of momentum from CDS and PPP, so I studied my buns off. I mastered the vignettes inside and out. I memorized all types of site planning data and information, and rocked all my practice exams. I felt great walking into that exam and was also proud of how hard I prepared for the test.

When I started the exam, many of the questions weren't even slightly geared toward Site Planning and Design—and if they were, they were outside of what I studied. I had several calculations that I wasn't prepared for, and as I moved through the multiple choice questions, I was continually tagging them as WTF to review later.

When I got to vignettes, they were the hardest I had ever seen. I had practiced on every version of the vignettes I could get my hands on, and the vignettes on my exam were truly impossible to solve without making a fatal error. I had to choose the lesser of all the errors I was being forced to make. So I killed an extra tree.

When I got my result, I failed the multiple choice and passed the vignettes. UGH....

The second time I took Site Planning was completely opposite—it was a walk in the park. It was the easiest multiple choice I ever answered. In fact, it was so easy I thought it was a joke. The vignette was very close to the NCARB practice version and I passed that exam with flying colors.

Nothing I could have done could have prepared me for the first time I took Site Planning and Design.

Rescheduling fine print

I failed Building Design and Construction Systems because my test was on a Tuesday, and I tried to reschedule on Thursday. The fine print says you cannot reschedule 0-3 days before the exam. I didn't realize it was BUSINESS DAYS, not calendar days. DUH! And for some reason, I also thought that because you can take a test on a Saturday, maybe that was considered a business day. But it's not.

I took the test anyway, definitely unprepared. Funny thing is that I actually did waaay better than I ever thought I would.

This is the dumbest reason ever to fail. Don't be a fool like I was.

The Good News

Honestly, the worst thing that can happen is you will lose your text exam fee, and you cannot retake the exam for six months. That's the worst of it. Luckily, I have also learned that there are a few positives in failing an exam. Focusing on these will help you for round two.

You now have feedback from your failed exam

Your test result will tell you what areas of the exam you failed. Check out the previous chapter, "Reading ARE Test Scores," for a more detailed look at how to decode your test results.

Take this information really seriously, and bone up on that information. Maybe you should add in a specialty book on that subject when you re-study.

When I failed Building Systems, my results said I had minor deficiencies in plumbing.

For round two, I focused on the MEEB plumbing chapters and watched several plumbing videos.

Need a recommendation for some new study material? Check out my Resources page at **YoungArchitect.com/ARebook** for reviews of the best study materials you've never heard of (or, at least, haven't tried yet).

Keep the old stuff, but study new materials for round two

When I failed Structural Systems, I studied Ballast and Kaplan extensively. The second time studying I avoided all study materials that I used from the first time, until I got to the final push. During the two weeks before my exam, I reviewed all of the study materials from the first time around. Having been schooled elsewhere, the old study materials had a whole new meaning, and I was able to benefit from them immensely.

You're not starting from ground zero

Luckily, you have already invested some time in this exam, so getting up to speed shouldn't take that long. Accept the fact that you're just gonna have to study more. See it as an opportunity to learn more about that topic, instead of a death sentence.

You're normal

It's normal to spend 2-4 years finishing the Architect Registration Exam.

These tests are really tough, and it's normal to not pass all seven the first time you take them. It's normal to not be an expert on all seven exams.

It's normal to fail an exam.

What isn't normal is finishing all seven exams in less than a year. It's not normal to think, "These tests aren't a big deal." If you need to make a living, have a relationship, or desire living a "normal life," you probably can"t finish them in such a short period of time.

NCARB does a great job of highlighting people who finished the exams in less than one year. I don't know anyone who has done that and only read about them from NCARB's marketing material. Sure, these people exist, but there aren"t as many of them as NCARB wants you to think.

Don't beat yourself up

It's not a big deal. You have done a lot of hard work to get to this point. Many people never do this, and the fact that you are studying and taking these tests is commendable.

The true meaning of failure is **giving up** after you have been handed a setback. Failure isn't failing a division of the ARE because you screwed up a calculation.

Keep studying … you're almost there. You have worked your butt off to get to this point.

I reframed failing the exam.

No one had publicly spoken about failing this exam until I wrote the post this chapter is based on. I've included a link to that post on my Resources page at **YoungArchitect.com/ARebook**.

You didn't fail the exam. You didn't fail anything. You aren't a failure.

You didn't pass because you weren't ready to. You just need to study up on a few more areas—no big deal. Each exam has so much material to study that it"s impossible to master it all.

When you revisit it later, it won't take you long to get up to speed, and you can now bone up on all the material you just didn't get to the last time around.

I convinced myself that I was going to keep taking the exams until I passed them all. Giving up wasn't an option. Don't let a small setback derail your dream of becoming a Licensed Architect!

Check out the previous chapter, "Reading ARE Test Scores," which will help you to identify areas that you need to study.

Reading ARE Test Scores

Let's be honest... The only reason you care about your Architecture Registration Exam test scores is because you failed the exam.

If you passed, who cares about your ARE test scores? There is no score; it's called "Pass."

A few months ago, I wrote a blog post about failing the architecture registration exam. I've posted a link to the blog post on my Resources page at **YoungArchitect.com/ARebook**. Since I wrote that post, several people have come back to me and said:

What are you talking about, Mike? What do you mean study more on the sections I failed?! How do I know what I failed?

After NCARB tells you that you failed, they also issue a document stating what areas of the exam you didn't do so hot in.

NCARB used to send all ARE test results in the mail, and around the end of 2013 they started doing it online. This is one of the big changes to the process that I applaud NCARB for.

However...

It has come to my attention that some of my readers are not actually getting this information.

The wait ...

NCARB used to say it took 2-4 weeks to get test results, and I think it only arrived in two weeks once. It usually took 3-6 weeks.

One of the worst parts of taking the ARE was spending the weeks after taking the test worrying if I passed or not. I wouldn't think about the ARE all day long, but every day when I got home from work, I got a rush of anxiety as I walked into my apartment building and checked the mailbox while I was waiting on my test results.

You can alleviate post-test anxiety somewhat by using my checkmark method that is discussed more thoroughly in the "Test Day Tips" chapter. But, I often didn't have my test results until at least 60 days after the exam, which is now the time you have to wait to retake an exam if you happen to fail. Kudos to NCARB for making this change.

Finding your test scores

Here is the process for downloading your score reports:

1. **Log into NCARB;**
2. **Click "NCARB Record";**
3. **Click "ARE" tab;**
4. **Click "My Examination" blue button; and**
5. **Download Score Report.**

I also believe the test scores are posted on the Web site several hours before an email is sent out saying, "Go get your results."

OK, let's take a look…

The test results that I am using for this example were shared with me by one of my awesome readers. I wiped out all their personal information and put my notes in red.

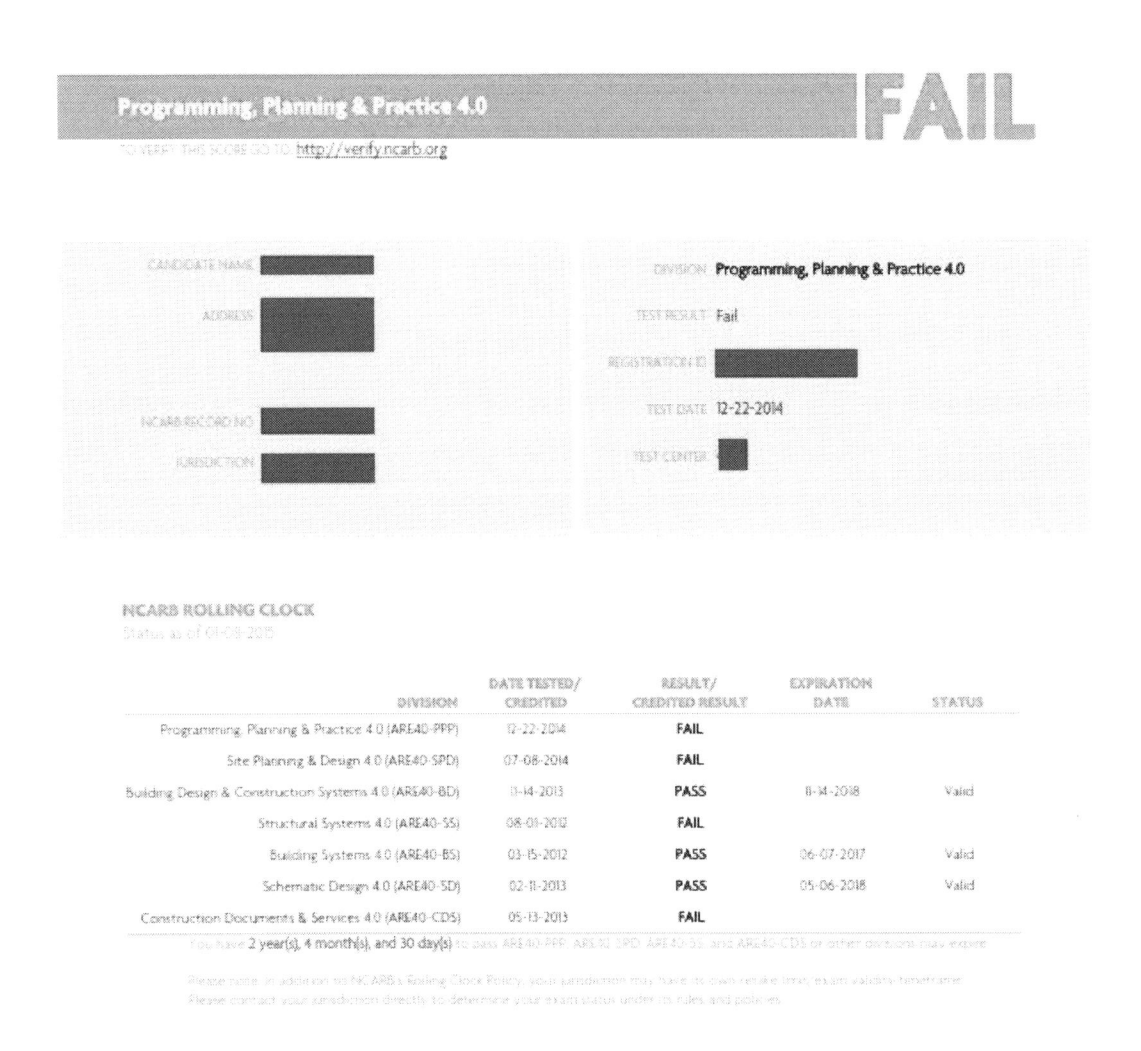

How To Pass The Architecture Registration Exam

Page 1 is pretty standard—test date information with that big ugly blue fail at the top.

How To Pass The Architecture Registration Exam

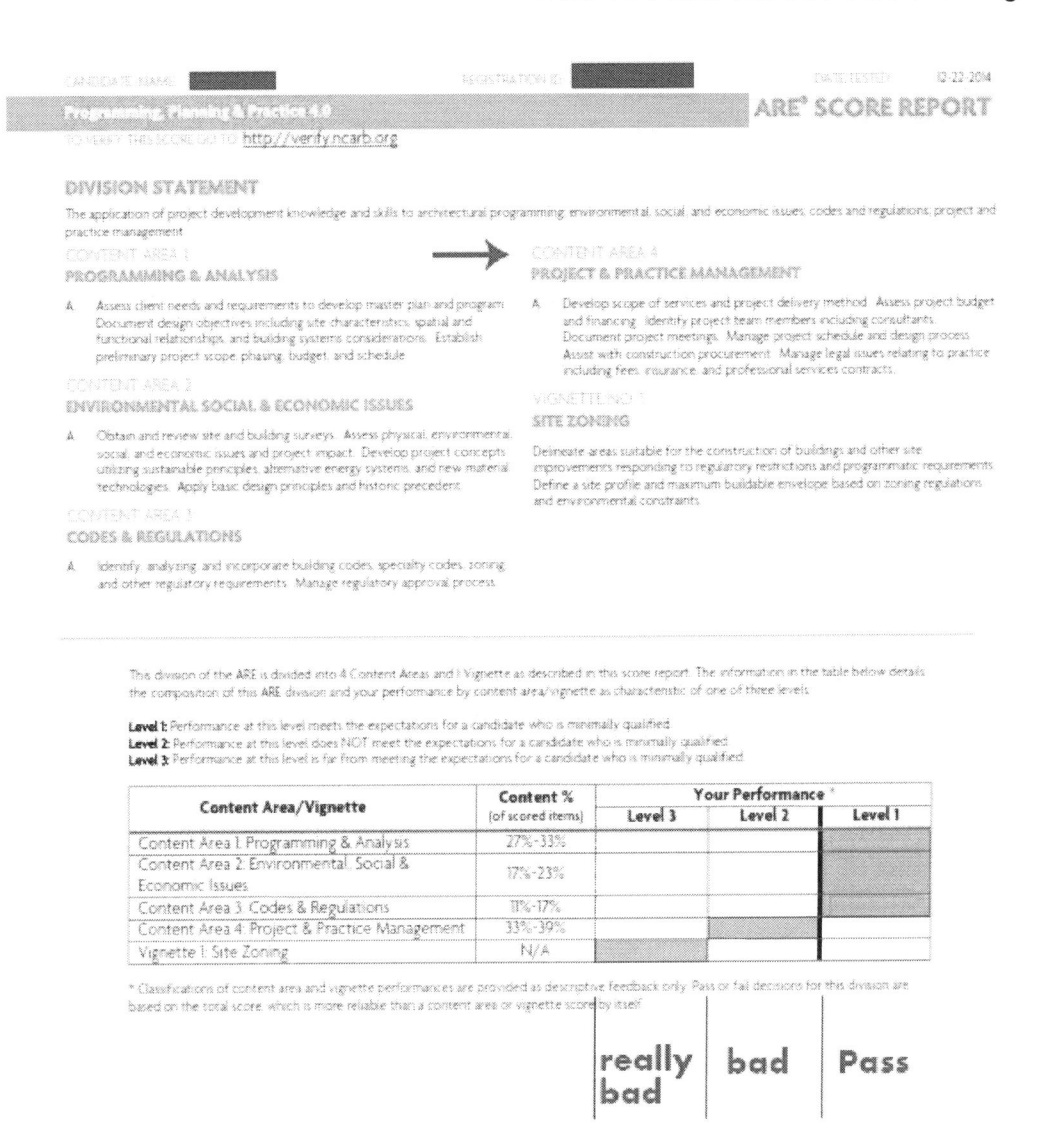

Page 2 is where all the juice is.

I apologize this graphic isn't larger and easier to read.

On the left hand side of the chart are the ARE content areas that you were tested on, and above the chart is a description of what falls under those content areas.

On the right side of the chart, it grades you on each content area.

How To Pass The Architecture Registration Exam

So this candidate failed the Site Zoning vignette and Content Area 4: Project & Practice Management.

As far as the vignettes go, NCARB doesn't elaborate on why you failed the vignettes. There is plenty of information available regarding how to pass the vignettes. I listed many of them on my guide, The Ultimate list of ARE Study Materials Part 3 – The Vignettes, which can be found on my Resources page at **YoungArchitect.com/**.

The Content Area 4 is a little trickier, but luckily the description above states that content as:

CONTENT AREA 4: PROJECT & PRACTICE MANAGEMENT

Develop scope of services and project delivery method. Assess project budget and financing. Identify project team members including consultants. Document project meetings. Manage project schedule and design process. Assist with construction procurement. Manage legal issues relating to practice including fees, insurance, and professional services contracts.

I know what you're thinking: "OK. Cool. Now I know what to study for next time. I am going to stop reading this now."

But, wait! There's more …

I don't know if you noticed, but the descriptions of the content areas on the ARE results page are awfully short. They are actually an abbreviated version of the content area description.

To find out what you need to study, you really need to go back to where the content areas of the exam are listed in the NCARB Study Guide.

If you pull up the same category, you get a much more thorough description of what content falls under Content Area 4.

CONTENT AREA 4: PROJECT & PRACTICE MANAGEMENT

Develop scope of services and project delivery method.
Assess project budget and financing. Identify project team members including consultants. Document project meetings. Manage project

schedule and design process. Assist with construction procurement. Manage legal issues relating to practice including fees, insurance, and professional services contracts.

1. Project Delivery & Procurement Methods
Determine the delivery and construction procurement method based on client requirements.

2. Project Budget Management
Determine fiscal requirements and apply appropriate methodology and techniques to manage project budgets.

3. Project Schedule Management
Establish and manage the professional service schedules for the project.

4. Contracts for Professional Services and Contract Negotiation
Determine, negotiate, execute, and manage the professional services agreements for the project.

5. Risk Management and Legal Issues Pertaining to Practice and Contracts
Assess and manage risk and legal issues related to the business and practice of architecture.

That's a little easier to understand than the short paragraph on the test results page. Some content areas have significantly more information in the ARE Study Guides.

And just for fun, you should also look at the information from ARE 3.1, which was retired a long time ago, but can be very valuable when studying for ARE 4.0 exams.

I've included links to all the ARE Study Guides and the ARE 3.1 material on my Resources page, at YoungArchitect.com/AREbook.

Spending time to understand what each content area is and how much it is worth is certainly not a waste of time, especially after you have failed an exam.

It's very important that you stay positive and don't allow yourself to get destructively discouraged. If you need some encouragement, revisit the previous chapter "Failing the Exam." Rebuilding your momentum and your test-taking confidence is going to take some time and effort, but you CAN do it!

Part 6
Arriving

Now That You're Finished…

You made it! You are now a Licensed Architect. Congratulations!

Now that the ARE is in your rearview mirror, you've got your whole life and career in front of you … and a whole lot more free time!

After I finished my exams, I encountered a few (minor) professional surprises. To better prepare you for professional life after the ARE—and to help you transition into your new role of Licensed Architect—I'm going to share a few lessons that I learned.

Be Aware of Extra Requirements

The state of Oregon, where I live, requires that all Licensed Architects take an extra test called the Jurisprudence Exam. Luckily, it's open book—and you can take it online.

The entire exam is about the laws that deal with having, using and maintaining an architecture license. Basically, the test breaks what is legal and what isn't. Essentially, if you do not maintain an active architecture license and practice without it, you will be penalized.

Compared to the AREs, the test wasn't that hard. It was really more of an exercise to make sure you read and understood the rules you have to follow as a Licensed Architect. Looking back, I think the Jurisprudence Exam makes a lot of sense.

The state of Oregon also requires an oral interview as the very last step of the Architecture Licensing process. The Oregon Board of Architect Examiners only offers the interview every other month. When I arrived for my interview, there were seven other candidates in the waiting room. Ironically, I even knew a few of them.

The interview was really nothing more than an opportunity for the licensing board to make sure we were real people and to say congratulations on arriving at this point. They met with us as a big group and we discussed some of the laws that were referenced in the Jurisprudence Exam. Looking back, taking the jurisprudence exam and meeting the Oregon Architecture board was a worthy experience. Not sure why all states don't have a similar process.

I suggest you research the specific requirements for architecture licensing in your state. I would hate to see you neglect to fulfill a state licensing requirement in your post-ARE daze of happiness and accomplishment.

Getting the Stamp… Physically

After I received my state license information, I purchased my stamp from Amazon. The process was so easy and painless. I highly recommend it.

All I had to do was email them all the information. They already had templates of every state to create architecture stamps, so they just populated it with my information and mailed it to me. Visit my Resources page at **YoungArchitect.com/AREBook** for a link to the location on Amazon where I purchased my stamp.

American Institute of Architects Membership

The American Institute of Architects (AIA) promotes free AIA convention admission to new members. Because of this great offer (a $675 value!), joining seemed like a no-brainer after I had my license in hand.

Not so fast—I once again learned the hard way that you have to read the fine print.

After I joined the AIA for the year, I found out that I did not qualify for the free convention registration, because I was a former member whose membership has been inactive for less than five years.

I later learned that I last joined the AIA four years and nine months earlier as an Associate member for the sole purpose of attending their ARE classes. At the time, an AIA Associate membership was around $100. However, because my one-year AIA Associate membership wasnt lapsed for more than five years ago, I was not eligible for the free convention ticket.

Had I known this, I would not have waited 6 months to join the AIA as a newly Licensed Architect. And no, I didn't end up going to the convention anyway.

Using the Stamp vs. Having the Stamp

I have used my stamp several times since I got it. Each time, it was for a small residential project for which I did 100 percent of the work. I felt very comfortable with each situation and even with the builder that was doing the work.

At the time, I was not carrying any professional insurance. They really were one-off projects, but I don't see myself using the stamp much more without carrying any insurance. There's just too much risk.

I currently work as a Facilities Project Manager for the City of Portland, Oregon. The fact that I am the Licensed Architect in our group comes up almost daily. I do drawings all the time for various projects and handle most of the architecture-related tasks of our group. The city has never asked me to use my stamp on any of my projects; however, I wouldn't even if they did ask.

Why not, you ask?

1. Having and using my architecture stamp isn't a part of my job description;
2. They didn't help me to pay for it or maintain it; and,
3. They aren't paying me enough to use my stamp.

It's important to the city to have licensed architects on staff, but if a project needs to be stamped, I will hire a local architect who is set up with all the right insurance to take on the liability.

After you have your stamp, please please please do not use it unless:
1. Your company is compensating you appropriately;
2. You have the opportunity to review and accept responsibility for all the work that you are stamping; and
3. You feel good about the project.

The Rest of Your Journey

By becoming a Licensed Architect, you have completed a very long process that probably started sometime in your early childhood with your first set of Legos. Take a minute to reflect on your accomplishments. Breathe. Congratulate yourself. Do something AWESOME to celebrate.

You have closed the ARE chapter of your life and career and have so many good things to look forward to in the future. No matter where your career or personal life may take you, you can always feel proud of passing the ARE.

I hope that this book helped you to along the way. I am genuinely interested in hearing your feedback, so don't be shy! Visit **YoungArchitect.com/AREBookTestimonial** to let me know what you liked and disliked about the book—and how it can be improved for future Licensed Architects.

So, now that your post-ARE partying is done, what's your next move?

As the months and years pass, don't forget to keep in touch with me on my blog at YoungArchitect.com and social media. I can't wait to hear about all the great things that you are working on!

Sincerely,

Michael Riscica

Made in the USA
San Bernardino, CA
25 March 2016